5
SPIRITUAL
SOLUTIONS
for Everyday
Parenting Challenges

5
SPIRITUAL
SOLUTIONS

for Everyday
Parenting Challenges

Richard and Linda Eyre

DESERET
BOOK

Salt Lake City, Utah

To our nine noble children—now all better adults than we
(and to those who are parents—better at that too)

Library of Congress Cataloging-in-Publication Data
Eyre, Richard M.
  5 spiritual solutions for everyday parenting challenges / Richard and Linda Eyre.
    p. cm.
  Includes bibliographical references and index.
  ISBN 978-1-60641-933-5 (hardbound : alk. paper)
  1. Child rearing. 2. Parenting. 3. Spiritual life—The Church of Jesus Christ of Latter-day Saints. I. Eyre, Linda, author. II. Title.
  HQ769.3.E97 2011
  248.8'450882893—dc22   2010047045

Printed in the United States of America
Worzalla Publishing Co., Stevens Point, WI

10 9 8 7 6 5 4 3 2 1

CONTENTS

CONTENTS

FOREWORD
Stephen R. Covey

Let me tell you some things about my friends, Richard and Linda Eyre, that will help you to better understand and appreciate what they have to say in this remarkable book.

They spent the first two years of their marriage in Boston where Richard was going to the Harvard Business School and Linda was teaching music. Then they moved to Washington, D.C., and helped found one of the nation's premier political consulting firms and planned and managed the campaigns of several U.S. senators and governors, including Utah's Senator Jake Garn. Richard had decided that politics was the place to make his contribution, and he was preparing to run for Congress when the Church called him to serve as mission president in London. Richard had just turned thirty-one and Linda was twenty-eight. They brought four small children with them to England, and returned with six. During the mission, the Eyres became convinced that the biggest problems and dangers in the world were not political, not economic, not even religious.

What endangered the world most, they began to believe (and what most threatened the Lord's plan), was the decline of families.

Returning home, they made a drastic career change. They closed down their consulting company and began writing and speaking to parents about ways to better prioritize and balance their lives and to build stronger and more lasting families. Over the next few years, the Eyres started Joy Schools, were named by President Reagan to direct the White House Conference on Parents and Children, and saw one of their books, *Teaching Your Children Values*, climb to #1 on the New York Times Bestseller list.

They also founded what may be the most complete parenting website ever created, www.valuesparenting.com, and developed a mission statement that they hoped would direct and motivate everything they and their company did: *FORTIFY FAMILIES by Celebrating Commitment, Popularizing Parenting, Bolstering Balance, and Validating Values.*

The Eyres knew, of course, that their efforts were a mere drop in the bucket, and that it would take voices much larger than theirs to combat the ever-growing attacks and undermining of family that seemed to gain momentum by the day. But through the hundreds of parenting programs and presentations they have made across America and in nearly fifty countries around the globe (often assisted now by one of their nine children), Richard and Linda have become even more convinced of what they knew all along: *That the real answers and the real help that parents need is not found in parenting methods or techniques, but in the perspectives and insights of the restored gospel and the plan of salvation.*

They have told me how many times they have found themselves concluding a parenting presentation to a group of Muslims in the Middle East, or a room of Hindus in India, or to Protestants and Catholics in Australia or England and wanted so badly to go on past the parenting ideas and tell them things that could truly transform their families . . . that their children are actually their spirit brothers and sisters . . . that God is literally their Father . . . that there is a divine, family-centered plan and purpose for this mortality . . . that there is a Church that can support and supplement their parenting with programs and doctrines that can save their children from the secularism and mischief of this world. I identify with this because I have felt those same longings.

And that is why it is a pleasure for me to help introduce what I think is the first parenting book that is based entirely on the eternal perspectives of the Restoration.

I believe, with the Eyres, that the thing that will make the biggest difference in our families is not the parenting expertise we may learn, but simply our ability to remember who our children really are, to recall what we know about how Heavenly Father parents us, and to use the insights of the Spirit along with the power of the priesthood to guide us along the perilous path of parenting in this pernicious world.

Every LDS parent should read this book! It is a truly unique and new kind of parenting approach, written on a spiritual level for parents who know what the world knows not.

PROLOGUE

Somewhere, a mom is nearing the end of a very bad, horrible, perfectly rotten day . . .

Now if I can just get these three into their car seats one more time and if they will just watch the Dora DVD for fifteen more minutes, I will be able to pick up Emily from the orthodontist and Jacob from his after-school detention and make it home in time to throw something on the table before Phil gets home from the office.

Spilled milk, detention, crooked teeth—these everyday hassles seem so small and insignificant now, compared to the phone call from the doctor yesterday morning. Early onset diabetes. Sarah, only 4 years old. It will change everything: our schedule (well, what we had of one), our diet, probably even the trip we've been planning for the summer.

I feel so helpless. I felt that even before this. Now it seems more hopeless than helpless. I hope it's okay to pray while driving, because that's all I can do now.

The words flood into my mind now as I pray, and I feel warmer, calmer. *Help me, Father. These five children are really your children and I love them more than life itself, but I am overwhelmed. I don't know what to* do. I don't know them like you do. I don't know what they need sometimes. *Experience, trial, patience, heartache, hope—this is what we signed up for, isn't it, Father? It's all part of the plan. You are there; your Spirit is here. They are your children and my channel to you in their behalf is direct; the connection is always live. I'm not alone. I can do this.*

We are anything but alone, physically or spiritually. We can do this. We chose to do this. Life is real!

Somewhere else, there is a dad in the middle of the night . . .

I've got an early morning meeting downtown, an important one, and here it is almost 2 a.m., and it's the third time this screaming baby has woken me up. Not wet, doesn't want the bottle, not tired, just mad that I won't play with her. She's going to wake her brother!

Trying to protect Barb, who's not feeling well, pregnant again. I've got to get some sleep. What am I going to do? Kids make life so crazy! I can't believe we're going to have three of them in a few months! What were we thinking? What have we gotten ourselves into? Stop crying, will you? Please, just stop!

I slump down in the chair, close my eyes, and say a little prayer . . . about helping this kid settle down. Exhausted, her little head lays on my chest, and for a moment she is quiet. I stroke her moist, tousled hair, and my prayer shifts toward thanks. Then the Spirit comes, bringing perspective into this little starlit bedroom. *This is my sister. I just happened to come to earth twenty-eight years ahead of her. It could be reversed. She could be my mom, holding a screaming little me.*

My praying mind opens up a little. *Parenting was God's role once, only His. We get to do it so we can become a little more like Him. It makes our life hard and deep. It drives us nuts, but it also makes us strong and good.*

Maybe I can do it a little more like He does it. Maybe I can use His power more, and His Spirit. Maybe He will whisper more to me, like this. After all, they're His children!

In another place, a mom sits with her bishop, her head in her tear-stained hands, seeking hope when there seems to be none . . .

"So you still haven't heard from him?"

"No, Bishop, not since the letter, and it's been more than a month now."

"And it was just an e-mail, no way to trace it?"

"None, and the police won't help since he's eighteen and has a right to go wherever he wants. Oh, Bishop, what are we going to do? I know he is doing drugs, and that's why he stole my money. Where did we go wrong? We raised him the same as the other two. Why? Why?"

The bishop takes her hand, pats it, and mumbles, "So you have pretty much given up then?"

Suddenly there is a change, in the air, in the feeling. The mom wipes her tears and straightens up, her eyes taking on a new look, stronger, almost fierce. "Given up?" she almost shouts. "I will never give up. That boy is my son. I don't know why God sent him to us, but there is a reason; I know there is. I will never give up!"

The bishop, feeling determination and devotion replace her despair, is strengthened by it and he offers words of encouragement to her, words that seem to come to him from somewhere else: "You are right! We never give up, and we are never helpless. We can pray. We can keep ourselves righteous and in tune. With our eternal perspective, the only way to fail as a parent is to give up." With a steady voice of authority, he adds, "And now I know that you will never do that."

PERSPECTIVES
Worldly Challenges, Spiritual Solutions

Do we as LDS parents, fully appreciate the parenting advantages we have within the restored gospel, within the Church? Do we remember and apply the insights and use what we know in the practical everyday challenges of raising our children? Do we grasp how great our spiritual solutions are and how powerful they can be as we face the never-greater challenges of raising righteous children in perilous times?

TEACHING AND LEARNING FROM THE PARENTS OF THIS PLANET

It's not just we and you who share the remarkable similarity of parenthood. Parents throughout the world, regardless of their culture, their religion, their politics, or their demographic or economic situation, are remarkably similar when it comes to their hopes, their dreams, and their worries for their children. Parents the world over, when they think of their families and their parenthood and their children and the extraordinary kind of love that attends those family relationships, find a commonality and kindred feeling that in many ways supersedes any other differences.

Over the last few years, we have traveled the world meeting with parents on every continent and in every imaginable situation. And, more often than not, we have learned as much as we have taught. There are good parents everywhere—striving parents, concerned parents, parents worried about the same things we worry about, and parents looking for deeper and better and more lasting solutions to the challenges they and their children face.

Whenever we address parents in some far corner of the world, we realize that most parents everywhere have as strong a desire as we do to raise happy, responsible kids and to build a strong, lasting family.

> ❦
>
> *Most parents everywhere have as strong a desire as we do to raise happy, responsible kids and to build a strong, lasting family.*
>
> ❦

Of course there are a lot of secular and worldly families who seem to worship the material gods of money and possessions, and there will never be any scarcity of the kind of abdicating parents who don't seem to feel much responsibility at all for their children. But there are also truly marvelous parents and families everywhere we go. These are the people we are most often with—since they are the type who attend discussions on parenting.

So when we speak, it is anything but a one-way street. We try to teach what we know, but we also marvel at what people already know and practice and at how much better they are at doing many family things than we are.

We can learn so much from other parents and other family cultures. In some parts of the world, families have such great respect for their elders and for their ancestors. In other cultures, parents are much better than we are at giving attention for positive behavior and largely ignoring little negative things that they don't want their kids to repeat.

In many other countries, parents seem to stay rooted and bonded with their extended families far better than more mobile and independent parents in the United States. In other places, followers of other religions are very devout, and in many developing countries there are humble households where there is a peace and tranquility that we find ourselves longing for.

So many Christian parents with whom we speak have a deep orientation to and a concentration on Jesus Christ. Perhaps it is because they do not have the restored gospel and the completely constituted Church in their lives that they are able to simplify and focus so completely on the thing they know best of all: Christ lives, and He is their Redeemer. We love it when we meet parents who base their whole lives and all their decisions, large and small, on the question, "What would Jesus do?"

We wish there were enough time (or pages in this book) to tell you all we have learned (and all we have felt) from parents in different parts of this world. To show our appreciation to them, we will share just a few of the experiences we have had with some of these good parents and the concerns and feelings they have for their families and their children, in particular.

• A Korean mother gets ready to leave her homeland to live with her two daughters at a boarding school in America so they can learn English and have a chance for a better life.

• A Saudi family sits outside their desert house in the cool of the evening and talks with us about how they hope they can send their children away to college without having them lose the values they have been taught.

• A Muslim family in Bahrain explains that their ten-year-old thinks he is old enough to understand and participate in the extensive daily fasting that accompanies the religious holiday Ramadan.

• A Japanese mother ignores her misbehaving child until he settles down and politely asks for her attention, whereupon she stops her conversation with us and directs it fully at her little boy.

• A group of successful businessmen in England decide to devote a full year to becoming better fathers to their children, and they print a booklet starting with the quote, "The one time I feel that I am a true man is when I am striving to be a good father to my children."

• Proud parents and friends watch as a young boy in Istanbul does an exercise with us on making decisions in advance. We give him a situation where there is a lot of peer pressure to try drugs and ask him what he will say. Standing tall, this little fellow says, "I would ask them if they wanted me to break a promise I made to myself when I was twelve years old."

• A group of mothers in Kenya talk, as they carry river water in pots on their heads back to their village, about their children and how to get them to be more obedient and show more respect.

• Chinese parents in Shanghai worry about how spoiled and entitled their child is becoming since there are six adults hovering over him all the time (two parents and four grandparents in a society that only allows one child).

• A distraught father in Bangkok bemoans the fact that his daughters are exposed to a sexually promiscuous society that goes against everything he believes about chastity and fidelity.

• The Malaysian Minister of Higher Education in Kuala Lumpur discusses his idea to have a mandatory class for first-year college students on marriage and parenting, "because our country will rise or fall based on the strength of our families."

• A Canadian banker sets up a "family economy" within his own home to teach his kids that money has to be earned, and that it grows when it is saved. "I want to put four or five kinds of currency in our family bank, so that my kids will realize that money works the same all over the world."

• A Kansas City owner of a countertop company explains that his children did not pay much attention to their family laws until he had them etched into a slab of granite that now stands in the front hallway of his home.

• A father in Texas loses his twelve-year-old daughter to leukemia just before Christmas, yet he glows with vibrant Christian faith that some day they will be reunited.

• Parents in Los Angeles brainstorm about the best way to "unspoil" their kids and find ways that they can give service rather than money to the poor people in their very own city.

THE SEARCH FOR SPIRITUAL ANSWERS

Obviously, LDS parents are not the only ones looking for real answers to our troublesome everyday parenting challenges. Nor are we the only ones seeking *spiritual* solutions. Not by a long shot! Many years ago, we started ending our secular parenting presentations with some fairly general spiritual thoughts on prayer and faith and having an eternal perspective. For every person who comes up after and says (like a fellow in Texas one night), "Hey, bub, I didn't pay good money to come here tonight and hear you talk about God," there are at least ten others who say something such as, "You really reached me when you started talking about prayer and the Spirit."

Wherever we go, we are always accompanied by the same two sentiments. First, we feel a *natural love for fellow parents*. Nothing makes you love other people faster than talking with them about their children and realizing how hard they are trying despite difficult circumstances and the influences of media and peer pressure that seem to work against all parents everywhere. And second, we feel a *longing* to be able to tell these good people eternal truths about who their children really are, what plan and purpose God had in sending them, and the personal help He will give us as we raise them.

THE UNIQUENESS AND IMPORTANCE OF OUR RESTORED INSIGHTS

As LDS parents, we share the same challenges, face the same onslaughts from the world as other parents. But through the restored gospel, which we treasure, we know so many additional truths about the origin, purpose, and destiny of families.

Should what we know about our children and about our families make a major difference in how we parent, and in how effective we are in raising children who are happy and faithful? Can the things we know connect to the everyday issues and challenges of raising responsible and moral kids in an irresponsible and amoral world?

We were once asked what we thought was the most distinctive and amazing insight or perspective of the Restoration. The question came in writing, and requested a one-page answer. Here is what we wrote. As you read it, think how astounding this doctrine is!

Perhaps one of the most remarkable and distinctive beliefs of The Church of Jesus Christ of Latter-day Saints is that God has revealed information and insight that was lost about His plan for mankind, and about the family-centered purpose of this mortal existence.

We believe that all of us once lived with our heavenly parents in a pre-mortal life before this world was. There, as God's spirit children, we developed and progressed until we were ready to enter this laboratory school of physical life. He knew us as individuals and sent us each into mortal circumstances where our challenges and opportunities would maximize our potential for growth. We understood, as spirits before coming here, that mortality would be full of risk and that pain and difficulty would be as much a part of it as the moments of fulfillment and joy.

This mortal sojourn on a physical planet where we could learn by our experience and our agency was a key part of God's plan for His family, and at its core was our opportunity to have and to live in families of our own where we could develop new levels of love, commitment, and sacrifice.

Thus we recognize babies who are born into this world as our spiritual siblings who come from our common home with God and who all already have distinctive personalities and characters developed during the course of their pre-earth existence. As our literal spirit brothers and sisters, children are worthy of our respect and diligent care, and parents are their stewards rather than their

> *The goal, in simple terms, is to return with our families to God's family and to be, upon that return, resurrected beings who are a little more like Him through the mortal experiences we have had and the choices we have made.*

creators—who should do their best to discover who and what their children already are and to raise them accordingly. In this context, prayer for help in understanding and raising our children is a direct appeal to the real Parent, who knows them (and us) perfectly.

The goal, in simple terms, is to return with our families to God's family and to be, upon that return, resurrected beings who are a little more like Him through the mortal experiences we have had and the choices we have made.

Since we believe that all mankind are literally brothers and sisters, searching out our ancestors and filling in and linking up our family trees is like doing the research and making the contacts for a massive family reunion.

In this everlasting perspective, marriage becomes profoundly important, as the beginning of a new family that will last forever, and that will be a subset of God's family. Thus, marriages performed in our temples are not "till death do us part" but "for time and all eternity." And no one is left out. All are part of families, of extended families, and of Heavenly Father's family. Those who, through life's circumstances, find themselves without children or a lasting marriage relationship will have those opportunities in a later sphere of existence.

Family is the core rather than the periphery. Children are the purpose rather than the sidelight. Work supports family rather than the other way around.

Because we see family life and commitment as central to life's experience and God's plan, the Church puts great effort and resources into the support of families. Programs and activities for children, youth, and families are extensive and absorb much of the resources, time, and energy of the Church's all-lay (volunteer) ministry. And for more than one hundred years, the Church has been gathering every genealogical and ancestral record available and made these available to any person anywhere who wants to trace his roots and connect to his broader family.

Everything is different with this perspective! We view earth differently. We view challenges differently. We view marriage differently. And perhaps most profoundly of all, we view children and our role as parents differently.

For us in the Church, family is the core rather than the periphery. Children are the purpose rather than the sidelight. Work supports family rather than the other way around. And the default switch on having children is ON rather than OFF—we assume we should, unless the Spirit tells us to wait, delay, pause, or stop. We consult with God about our family planning rather than doing whatever seems convenient or easy for us.

Sharing this spiritual perspective about children and families and eternity is, by the way, the best way to give context to why the Church takes the positions it does on certain moral and political issues. We have never once had anyone criticize our stand on abortion or gay marriage once they know about those spiritual perspectives and understand that procreation and eternal families are the core of our belief about life's purpose. They may not agree with us, and they may not ask for the missionaries, but they know where we stand, and they know *why* we stand there, and in the process of telling them, we have raised the level of the discussion from political to spiritual where arguments are harder to have and respect is easier to find.

REMEMBERING

In our LDS perspectives and programs lie genuine spiritual solutions. If we can only remember them . . . and rely on them . . . and remember to apply them . . .

Despite the beauty and insight of what we know about our children and about our stewardship over them, in the business of the day and the pressure of modern life, it is so easy to forget.

The key to better parenting is not only to remember what we know, but to remember to apply it.

"Remember" in the scriptures

> **Remembering**
> - "O, remember" —Alma (Alma 37:35)
> - "O remember, remember" —Helaman (Helaman 5:9)
> - "Remember, and always retain in remembrance" —King Benjamin (Mosiah 4:11)
> - "Remember, and always retain in your minds" —God to Joseph Smith (D&C 46:10)

9

is not a passive but an active word. It involves appreciating and applying and anticipating and being anxiously engaged.

In a complex world, we often respect complexity and distrust simplicity. Can something as simple as remembering be a solution?

Yes!

Because what we are remembering is eternal spiritual identity, and prayer that penetrates the veil, and the parenting patterns of God.

Remembering what the Restoration tells us about our children, about how God parents, and about our access to His power, His Church, and His Spirit should make us feel a stewardship-like humility, not a Rameumptom-like pride. Where much is given, much is expected. And, indeed, much is expected of us as LDS parents—by our children, and by their true Father.

WORRIES

But let's get back to the common, gritty, everyday problems of this crazy world we find ourselves in. What do you worry about most with your kids? What concerns sometimes keep you awake at night? What scares the daylights out of you or makes you want to tear your hair out? If you're like most parents, you can make up quite a list:

Pornography

Violence

Drugs

Alcohol

All of the above in movies and video games

Peer pressure

Bullying

Entitlement

Sexual experimentation

Sexual abuse

Too much time on the Internet

Excessive texting (and promiscuous "sexting")
Gender identification
Nutrition, weight, and eating disorders
Self-esteem
Friends and "bad friends"
Testimony
Desire to learn, motivation in school
Learning to work
Being responsible
Handling money
Grades
ADHD
Rudeness and disrespect
Sibling rivalries and jealousies
Dishonesty
Sharing and working with others
Obedience
Self-discipline
Safety
Making good choices
Caring about/being sensitive to others
Discovering talents and aptitudes
Staying on task, setting their own goals
Getting spoiled by grandparents
Growing up too fast
Insecurity
Not fitting in/feeling left out
Whining, complaining
Inactivity/not wanting to go to Church
Rebellion

How do you deal with these worries? Where do you look for answers?

Do you ask your friends? Read parenting books? Scan the Internet for answers in chat rooms or mommy blogs? (There is nothing wrong with any of these sources, and useful answers may be found.)

Or do you look to more spiritual sources? To the scriptures, to the words of prophets and Church leaders, and to our priesthood and Relief Society lessons? While we trust these spiritual sources more, they may not always give us the specifics we need or tell us exactly how to *apply* things with our own individual kids. In other words, there may be too much space between the general principles and the specific solutions to everyday problems that we so desperately need.

Our parenting issues and challenges sometimes feel so overwhelming and so unique to us that we wonder if anyone else has ever faced them, and we get so caught up in the world's solutions that we sometimes forget to turn to the Lord for solutions as fully as we should.

How can the gospel and the truths of the Restoration and the plan of salvation be applied directly and specifically to how we raise our children?

Our parenting issues and challenges sometimes feel so overwhelming and so unique to us that we wonder if anyone else has ever faced them, and we get so caught up in the world's solutions that we sometimes forget to turn to the Lord for solutions as fully as we should.

Yet all parents with spiritual convictions, even those not of our faith, yearn for deeper, more spiritual solutions. Recently we asked a Muslim father in Indonesia what his goal was for his children. Unaware that he was stating what I have always thought of as an LDS cliché, he said, "I want them to be able to operate successfully in the world, but not to be part of the world." He wanted, just as we all do, for his kids to be able to live happily and successfully in the world, but not be worldly. He wanted his children to be well-adjusted and comfortable, but to hold to higher, older values. As a parent, he wanted to apply spiritual solutions to worldly problems.

Don't we all! The difference is that we, because of the Restoration, have the incalculably valuable advantage of a clear and complete spiritual perspective. While parents everywhere may suspect such things, we *know* through our doctrine who our children are and where they came from. We know they are our spiritual brothers and sisters and that we are mere stewards over them here and that their true Father, and ours, is God. We know that they have been who they are for an eternity and that they come to us with preexisting personalities, gifts, and challenges. We know God as a personal spiritual Father and we know something of His parenting methods. We have in the Church an extensive and remarkable support system that is designed for the purpose of helping us teach our children the values of eternity and the principles of the gospel. Youth leaders, bishops, scout masters, home teachers, coaches, Sunday School teachers all surround us within a church that President Harold B. Lee called "the scaffolding" that helps us build eternal families.[1]

And if all that were not enough, we have the very power of God with which we can bless our children and the true gift of the Holy Ghost to guide us as to what they need and how each can best be raised.

How then can we fail?

The answer is, we can fail because there is such a disconnect between all these spiritual perspectives, blessings, insights, and supports and the day-to-day, down-and-dirty temptations, attitudes, media, and peer pressure that suck away at our children every day.

We can fail because we "forget to remember" what we know both about our children and about God's way. And we can fail because we often don't apply it even when we remember it.

So, how do we start applying spiritual solutions to worldly problems?

PERSPECTIVE

One night the captain of a tanker saw a light dead ahead. He directed his signalman to flash a signal to the light, which went: "Change course 10 degrees south."

The reply was quickly flashed back: "You change course 10 degrees north."

The captain was a little annoyed at this reply and sent a further message: "I am a captain. Change course 10 degrees south."

Back came the reply: "I am an able seaman. Change course 10 degrees north."

The captain was outraged at this reply and sent a message: "I am a 240,000-ton tanker. Change course 10 degrees south!"

Back came the reply: "I am a *lighthouse!* Change course 10 degrees north!"[2]

Perspective is everything. When we see things accurately, and within the bigger picture, when we "get it" and understand what is really happening and why, we can then figure things out and make good choices.

If you were driving along in the dark and could see only the turnings into cross streets and the forks in the road, you would be subject to all kinds of directional mistakes. But if you had your GPS and could see it all from above, adjusting your perspective to a mile, to five miles, to fifty miles, to the whole distance from where you are to where you want to go, you could then make all the right turns along the way.

The plan of salvation is the big picture, the big map that shows the destination, and the restored gospel is the clearly marked path. And the gospel GPS is so advanced that it allows for U-turns and course corrections as long as we don't turn it off or tune it out. And, like a buddy-tracking application, it also allows us to locate the position of our kids and to coordinate the journeys so that we all end up at the same place.

The trouble is, our kids are not driving on completed, perfect, or easy roads. There is a lot of construction going on out there, some huge potholes, even some steep cliffs without guardrails, so it's not enough to just tell them where we want them to go.

They might get there by trial and error, but that is such a painful and dangerous way to travel. We

> ❦
>
> *It is the gospel and its insights that help us find more GPS solutions and thus suffer through fewer trial-and-error dead ends.*
>
> ❦

need to somehow give them their own GPS and to show them how to use it well enough to negotiate roads that are, frankly, more difficult and dangerous than ours.

Still, if they really see the destination clearly, and if they understand how wonderful it is, and if neither we nor they ever give up on the GPS or on the renewal of course correction, they will get there, maybe not on exactly the route we imagined and maybe a little later than we would have liked, but they will get there.

It is the gospel and its insights that help us find more GPS solutions and thus suffer through fewer trial-and-error dead ends.

AWARENESS, APPRECIATION, AND APPLICATION

If you had to state the difference between God and man in one word, what word would you choose?

"Perfection."

"Completeness."

"Comprehension."

Each of those would be good answers. And how about "perspective"? We see and understand such a narrow slice, and God sees all, the

15

whole picture, all of space and all of time and all of eternity . . . and all of each of our souls.

> *A spiritual solution is a parenting approach that is based not on the philosophies of men but on the wisdom of God; it stems not from man's techniques but from Heavenly Father's doctrine and power.*

Another way of saying it might be "awareness." He is aware of all—of all laws, of all matter, of all possibility—and thus He is omnipotent, omniscient, and in a way omnipresent.

It follows, then, that the more aware we are, the more we are like God. If we want to model our parenthood after God's, we can begin by increasing our awareness. If He is aware of every sparrow that falls from a branch and of every atom in every particle and of every galaxy in the universe and of every thought in the mind of each of His children, we can move slightly toward being like him by striving to be more aware of who our children are and of where they fit in our families and in God's family.

WHAT ARE "SPIRITUAL SOLUTIONS"?

What, exactly, is a "spiritual solution" with our children?

In simple terms, it is a parenting approach that is based not on the philosophies of men but on the wisdom of God; it stems not from man's techniques but from Heavenly Father's doctrine and power.

When we apply gospel truth to parenting challenges, we come up with spiritual solutions.

Spiritual solutions are honest attempts to use God's truths, His power, His methods, and His love to be the best stewards we can of the children that He has entrusted to us.

Remembering and applying spiritual solutions is not easy, nor do any of them have any guarantees of short-term success.

Spiritual solutions must be applied with spiritual perspectives, which remind us that each child is different, each comes from an eternity of becoming whom he or she already is, each brings an already formed personality and set of gifts and challenges from the premortal life, each will test us and prove us in countless ways and will contribute as much to our growth and salvation as we do to his or hers, and each was given to us (as opposed to some other family) for real reasons known only to God.

And spiritual solutions are centered on Christ. Whether we are talking about His example or about His power, or about the programs of His Church, all true spiritual solutions stem from Him.

Spiritual parenting solutions are not the exclusive domain of LDS parents. They are available to any person of faith who seeks them. But the specifics of what LDS parents know make these solutions particularly clear and particularly available to those in the Church who seek them.

OFFENSE AND DEFENSE

Much parenting advice seems to come from the defense. "If you have this problem, try this technique" or "If Johnny does this, you do that." Reactive rather than proactive. Wait for the problem and then try to solve it. If you just looked at the title of this book you might think it was in that same mode—start with problems and look for solutions.

But because in the Church we know God's plan and because we know something of His goals for His children, we are better equipped to be proactive, to take the offense rather than the defense. So in each of the following five solutions, we will start with the principle or the insight and advantage we have via the gospel—the particular solution that is available to LDS parents.

Once we have discussed and thought together about the principle involved, along with the *insights* and perspectives it gives, we can get into some ideas for *applying* it and implementing it so that it becomes

17

a parenting solution. Then, last rather than first, we can think about the problems it can *impact* or help us with and the important and good things it can allow us to do with and for our children.

By the time you have thought about the insights and some examples of applications, you will be ready to look at your own situations, problems, and opportunities and where the solution can have an impact. When it comes to your own unique, one-of-a-kind children, you are the only parenting expert, and what you don't need is someone else telling you what your child's problem might be and how to apply some one-size-fits-all, cookie-cutter quick fix. We respect you too much as a parent to even try that. All we can do is list some examples of the kind of everyday issues that the spiritual solution could impact.

The key is for you to think about each spiritual solution, to remember it and keep it in mind, and to find your own ways to apply it to both the everyday challenges and the opportunities you see with your children and in your family.

So each solution will have three main sections:

Insights

Applications

Impacts

RELAX, REMEMBER, AND RELY ON CHRIST

One great key to spiritual parenting is to relax and trust God. Don't run faster than you can. Don't expect perfection. Don't expect immediate results on the new things you try. Be patient and enjoy the journey. Do not be overwhelmed. You can't implement every idea in this book. Don't even try! If you are like most parents, you are already close to capacity. Pick the things that appeal to you, that are right for your unique situation and your unique kids. And pick the ones that look like they will add to your joy, not diminish it.

And remember this: The beauty of spiritual solutions is that they don't completely depend on you! They rely on the Spirit, and on the priesthood, and on the Heavenly Father of us all, and they lift our burdens rather than make them heavier.

This does not mean that spiritual solutions don't take effort on our part, but they also hinge on faith and on powers far beyond ours. All true spiritual solutions ultimately rely on Christ, and His "yoke is easy, and [His] burden is light" (Matthew 11:30). "Cast thy burden upon the Lord" (Psalm 55:22), we are also told. Spiritual solutions are His solutions, and He IS the solution.

So while there are a lot of ideas and suggestions you find that you like, the most important part of each of the five spiritual solutions is simply remembering the principle and the perspective involved. *Remembering*, that's all.

All, but not easy. What's easy is to forget. The press and noise of the material world makes us forget the spiritual world. No wonder the Lord tells us so often to "remember." "Remember, and always retain

> *The beauty of spiritual solutions is that they don't completely depend on you! They rely on the Spirit, and on the priesthood, and on the Heavenly Father of us all, and they lift our burdens rather than make them heavier.*

in [your] remembrance" (Mosiah 4:11). Remember to remember. It is not enough to know, not enough even to know and understand. We must remember!

If we remember who our children really are, it will affect our parenting in countless positive ways, and only a few of them can be outlined in this book. If we remember what we know about how God parents us, it will influence us in ways we may not even be aware of. If we remember that we can appeal directly to the true Parent, that He will guide our efforts, and if we remember to depend on the Church, to use the priesthood and to follow the promptings of the Spirit and most of all to "always remember" the Savior, we will never have a parenting challenge we cannot meet, and we will never be alone.

SOLUTION
1
Remember Your Children's True Identity

❧

*Apply what we know about where our children came from . . .
and discover their unique eternal personalities.* Understand that
our children are actually our spiritual siblings, and we should respect
them as well as love them.

A young, somewhat nervous mom named Liz sat across a table from
us, baring her soul. (That happens sometimes when people view you as
parenting experts and hope that you will give them some kind of quick
fix for their worries about their kids.)

In this case, it wasn't a gradual process, with her revealing bit by bit
in response to our questions. She was a Southern gal, open and demon-
strative, and she just blurted it all out. All we could do for quite a while
was sit there and listen.

"I think I'm a pretty good mom, and heaven knows, I just love my
kids to pieces, all four of them. And they're good kids for the most part.
We've trained them, tried real hard to make them polite and present-
able and to do the right thing.

"But here's the thing, y'all, they're just all so different. Kendra, my fourteen-year-old, always makes me proud—she would just never, never do anything to displease me, and Betsy pretty much just follows her around, so she's no problem. But James, bless him, he's only eleven and he's like to drive me crazy. If there's just a speck of trouble anywhere he will find it, and get right in it! And he's reckless. Oh my, he is reckless. I sometimes wonder how he gets through a day in one piece. And he sasses me so much now—just no respect—and then Betsy hears him and she starts thinking it's okay to talk to me that way."

Liz went on and on, telling us about her perfectionist daughter and her rebellious son and her other troubles with each of her kids. She ended with, "Guilt, guilt, guilt! I blame everything on myself. Well, there's really not anybody else to blame, is there?"

We sat there listening, making a note once in a while, and waiting for her to take a breath so we could share some ideas and methods we thought might help here and there. But what we were inwardly *wanting* to tell her was Solution #1—we wanted to tell her who her kids really are and where they came from, and to give her an eternal context in which to try to understand her children and to figure out the best way to help each of them.

We have those same longings every single time we counsel with a parent who does not have the insights and the environment of the Church.

What we were wishing we could share with Liz and with so many others—had there been time and had they been interested—was what we can now share with you as a fellow member and a fellow believer in a restored eternal perspective.

INSIGHTS

Who Are You Really?

It's a question that comes up in movies sometimes—at climatic, sometimes romantic, moments.

Lois Lane has just seen something in Clark Kent that makes her wonder . . .

Or Vicki Vale is probing Bruce Wayne. Could he be Batman?

Or even Bella in the first Twilight movie, when Edward has just done something surprising or extraordinary . . .

Who are you really?

Is there something more to you than I know?

Are you actually from another place?

Do you have potential and power and gifts that I have not yet imagined?

Who are you really?

Another classic time the question is asked is by mothers, often new mothers, gazing deeply into the eyes of their infant, touched by the presence of this new one, sensing that this little spirit is much older than its few hours on earth.

Where did you come from?

What have you already become?

What gifts and talents are already developed, implanted, and waiting to be found in your soul?

Who are you really?

Parent or Sibling, Owner or Steward?

I was sitting quietly in our living room one Sunday after church, reading an article and enjoying a peaceful moment. Our five-and-a-half-year-old daughter Charity bustled in, pulled the magazine down from in front of my face, looked into my eyes, and made a shocking statement:

"You're not actually my Daddy!" (Is "actually" the favorite word of all precocious five-year-olds?)

"Now what do you mean by that, sweetheart?" I responded.

"Well," she said, "My Primary teacher taught us that Heavenly Father is our real Daddy . . . so you are really just my brother!"

I smiled and patted her little head and said, "That's exactly right,

Charity, and I am very happy to be your brother." I picked my magazine back up.

But she wasn't done yet. "Yeah, Dad, but guess what else? I actually think that you are actually my *little* brother and I am actually your *big* sister!"

"Really?" I stammered, trying now to remember who her Primary teacher was.

"Yeah, Dad, because my teacher said that probably Heavenly Father saved his most mature children to come down here last."

I laughed and patted her head again and then followed her with my eyes as she skipped out of the room, thinking that she was probably right.

The perspective of knowing who our children really are should change (and enhance) how we raise them more than any parenting method or technique ever could.

A simple thought, one that can be comprehended by a five-year-old child. But is there anything more profound? The perspective of knowing who our children really are should change (and enhance) how we raise them more than any parenting method or technique ever could.

Oh, how much that perspective should affect how we treat these little big sisters and little big brothers of ours!

The Third Variable

Have you heard the story of the boy who came home from school on report card day and sheepishly handed his not-so-good marks to his father?

The dad studied the document, and color started rising up his face. But before he could say anything, the boy, with an artful shrug of his shoulders and a palms-up gesture of dismay, said:

"Gee Dad, what do you think it could be, environment or heredity?"

The questions for us parents are, "How did our kids become who they are? Where did they get their personalities and their propensities? Why is it so hard to change them?"

The world has only two answers. As the boy said, "Heredity and environment." Genetics and training. Nature and nurture.

The problem with that binary answer is that it doesn't explain the differences. Two siblings from the same gene pool, raised in the same home, can be different in almost every way. Even twins. And it drives parents to distraction. Just when we think we have one child figured out ("I'm all practiced up for the next one"), along comes another one with whom nothing works the same!

Is there another, third variable? We know the answer, of course, and it is a huge one, probably more consequential than either of the other two. The biggest variable is eternity! The missing piece in the puzzle is the premortal life where each of our children began their journey and became who they are.

Lumps of Clay or Seedlings

As a brand-new, first-time mother in the delivery room, I remember being so thrilled at the prospect of doing my very best to mold the sweet little angel who had just emerged into the world into a wonderful individual. I had plans to make her into just the perfect balance of all that was admirable and good.

Now, after raising nine children, I have a whole new paradigm. I firmly believe the following: *They are who they are!* These beautiful people whom we joyfully greet and hold in our arms in the delivery room with eternity behind their eyes, come already intact with a distinct personality, certain gifts, and definite passions.

Knowing our children are our spiritual siblings and have been becoming who they are for the first side of eternity does not mean we cannot help them, teach them, improve them here in "middle earth." On the contrary, if we go about it lovingly and wisely, we can make a huge difference in the rest of their lives, not to mention the other side of their eternity.

But we need to understand that we are not starting from scratch. We are not their creators, or their makers, or their owners, nor are we fully responsible for all that they are.

One of the parenting analogies we never use is the one that says, "Children are lumps of clay, and parents are the sculptors."

Do you have any lumps of clay? We don't! Mold them into whatever we want them to be? We don't think so! First, they're not that malleable and second, even if you could make them into some perfect little image of clay that extended your own ego and caused you no trouble at all, would you really want to, knowing that they are unique children of God with their own destinies and foreordinations?

A much better analogy would be to liken children to seedlings in a nursery. You know how all the little plants look the same when they are just little green shoots? But until you stop to read the little label on each one, you don't know if it is an oak tree, a fir tree, or a lilac bush.

The fact is, we will never turn a pine into an oak; but the more we know about what each little seedling is, the better we can apply the right amount of water, the right kind of nutrients, and make it the best pine it can be.

And that should be our goal.

A Brief Fable in Which You Are the Adoptive Parent

Imagine that you were given the opportunity to adopt a child.

It was not a child of poverty or an orphan or a child needing help because she came from a dangerous or dysfunctional home.

Just the contrary. This child is the daughter of a king. He wants her adopted because he wants her to experience "real life" in a real home where she will experience all kinds of good things and bad things, all of the challenges and choices that will test her and cause her to progress and grow. In the king's own home, things are too easy and she did not face the opposition or the struggles that would help her prove herself and discover the deeper parts of herself.

And you are chosen to be the adoptive parent. You are overwhelmed by the honor and humbled by the responsibility.

You view the child as your first priority, you work at making her life full and real, you love her deeply and unconditionally, and you speak often to the king as you seek to know her better and to give her what the king would want her to have.

Do you see the elements of truth in this fable? Can we remember that our children are actually the children of the King?

Guilt and Pride, the Two Imposters: Getting Rid of Both

We were visiting a little ward in rural Idaho and the Sunday School lesson happened to be on parenting. We sat quietly and anonymously and listened.

There was another visitor there, kind of a sophisticated city slicker who seemed to have all the answers. (He also seemed to have perfect kids because he prefaced each comment he made with something such as, "Well, my son, the student body president . . ." or "The way I handled that with my daughter, the valedictorian . . .")

If it had just been a couple of times, it would have been fine, but about the sixth time he gave his perfect, pat answer about his perfect kids, you could almost hear the groans about this self-righteous guy who seemed to have no problems.

Then, just after the first bell, a small, quiet-voiced farmer raised his hand, stood up, and turned to face the man. "Excuse me," he said with a high-pitched country twang, "but God must notta thought much of you as a parent, sendin' ya all them *easy* kids."

There were some soft giggles from every direction and an almost audible murmur of agreement among the class members. We gave each other's hand a little squeeze and both mumbled, "Amen!" No offense was taken, but we all knew exactly what that good man was saying.

Knowing what we know about our children's premortal existence, about the eternity they have already spent becoming who they are, we had better not take too much credit for who they are.

And for the same reason, we had better not feel too much guilt for their imperfections and problems. . . .

Because that courageous little farmer could have also said, in another situation to another parent, "God musta thought quite a bit of you as a parent, sendin' ya that difficult kid."

> ∽
>
> *We didn't create our children; they come as who they are from a Father who entrusts us with stewardship for them.*
>
> ∽

Part of eternal-perspective parenting, and a big part of this first spiritual solution, is remembering and understanding that we didn't create our children, that they come as who they are from a Father who entrusts us with stewardship for them. We do our best to help our children grow and develop in ways that are uniquely right for them, and we seek God's help. Thus we try not to judge other parents or ourselves. We replace pride with gratitude when a child does something well or shows promise in some way, and we replace guilt with perspective and added love when a child falls short or makes a mistake.

Avoiding Like a Plague the Tendency to Judge and Compare

As equally counterproductive with guilt and pride (and as equally inconsistent with truths that we know) are judging and comparing.

It is so easy to look at another family (at church or on a blog) and see them as more organized, more in control, more *perfect* than we are!

First of all, it's not a fair comparison. Often you are comparing that family at its best to your family at its worst.

And the results of the comparing will almost always be

negative—discouragement for you and perhaps animosity or jealousy toward them.

The only thing worse than comparing is *judging.* And that is so easy to do.

"Look at that kid; he must not be getting a very good example at home!"

"From the looks of that family, they're not very in tune with the gospel."

"They really think they are special, don't they? They certainly think they are better than the rest of us."

The safer assumption (and the more loving one) is that pretty much every parent you know is doing the best he or she can, given what they know, who their kids are, and what other problems they have.

APPLICATIONS

After pondering our children's origin and relationship to God, the challenge is to apply the insights in our everyday parenting. The following applications come in batches—first about spiritual respect, then about figuring out our children's spiritual identity, and helping them to do the same, and finally about guiding them in the decisions that will affect who they become.

Giving and Receiving Spiritual Respect

There are not many things more unpleasant than listening to a kid mouth off, with complete disrespect, to his mother. The only thing that might rival it is hearing a parent yelling at a child with even less respect.

You hear it everywhere, in airports or grocery stores, in school yards or just walking down the street—parents yelling or barking or screaming or being sarcastic with their kids—parents who sound like drill sergeants or wardens in a prison. They show no respect and they treat their kids like slaves or imbeciles or like little jerks that are so irritating that they can hardly stand them.

Hearing a parent abuse a child verbally can be a painful, frightening thing as described by Nancy Baird in a BYU Women's conference presentation:

> One morning, very early, in Puerto Rico, I was out running in a little park in our "Urb," our gated neighborhood. As I ran, I heard through an open window in a house above me, a man screaming, raging at a child. It was a terrible sound. The screaming. The child crying.
>
> The park became silent. Which is saying something on an island where there is always sound—birds, wind, palms moving. There was no sound beside the screaming and the crying of the child. The birds stopped singing. The wind dropped. The palms were still. It was as though the whole world stopped and was listening.
>
> It says in D&C 38:11–12: "The powers of darkness prevail upon the earth, among the children of men, in the presence of all the hosts of heaven—Which causeth silence to reign, and all eternity is pained. . . ."
>
> This is exactly what happened in the park: Silence reigned in the face of the powers of darkness. Eternity was pained.
>
> It was frightening.[1]

When we as LDS parents disrespect our children, we are forgetting that they are our spirit brothers and sisters, and that they have placed unbelievable trust in us by coming, as helpless infants, into our homes and our care, hoping we will guide and teach and lift them toward happy adulthood.

We are forgetting that they could just as well be our parents!

Simply remembering and reminding ourselves of this can expand the respect we give them, and ultimately the respect they return to us.

This doesn't mean we don't discipline them, or correct them, or have high expectations of them. But it does mean that we try to do each of these things with gentleness, with perspective, with patience, and with respect.

You may not be (hopefully have never been) a *blatantly* disrespectful parent, one who verbally abuses your child in ugly and profane ways, but if we are not wary, disrespect creeps in through our tone of voice and even through the looks we give our children.

The DAT Formula

For solid, conscientious parents who do generally treat their children with respect but who would still like to improve, we recommend "the DAT formula."

D stands for decibels. Just turn down your volume a little, speak a little more softly, a little more calmly (most parents have learned that decibels are contagious, and that the louder they speak, the louder their children will respond, and vice versa).

The A is for agency. When we give children no choices or input on things, we disrespect them as spirits. Of course we have to make most choices for them when they are small, but giving them as many choices as we can, as early as we can (things as simple as what color of juice they want), is not only a great teaching method, but a simple and direct way of respecting them.

The T is for tone. Even when our decibels are OK, we often use a tone that is condescending or sarcastic or even mean or arbitrary—a tone we would never use with a friend or other person we respect.

"Let's Start Over"

Of course, the time when we are most prone to lose our respectful tone with our children is when they are disrespectful of us. How do we respect a sassy child, or an outright rude kid? Don't we need to immediately put them in their place? To come down hard on them? To make them afraid to ever say something like that again?

In fact, what we need to realize is that rudeness and disrespect in a child is usually just a bad habit. They are not black-hearted, hateful little people who are trying to hurt us. They have just heard rudeness, picked it up, and learned some bad habits from their friends or from the media (or from us!). The best way to break a bad habit is to set up a simple system that allows them to instantly correct themselves. We call it "starting over."

In a family home evening, do some role-playing where a parent or child is being rude or disrespectful. Then say, "What if every time that happened, the person whom we were being rude to just said, 'Let's start over.'" Then role-play the same situation but with both parent and child (or child to child) responding with respect.

Create other brief role plays from recent experiences and emphasize that after someone says, "Sorry, let's start over," both parties say what they have just said in a more respectful way.

Then, like all parenting efforts, it's a matter of consistency. Do the start-over every time there is rudeness, and invite children to do the same with you, or with their siblings. And start over as many times as it takes to get it right. And keep doing it until the bad habits are broken.

"Starting Over" Example

Mom says (somewhat sharply), "Get in here and take the garbage out."

Child says, "Leave me alone. Can't you see I'm doing my homework!"

Mom gets eye contact and says, "Sorry, let's start over. Will you please come and take the garbage out?"

Child says, "Yes, Mom, but is it okay if I just finish this one problem first?"

Apologizing

While we are talking about saying "sorry," let's point out that it is one of the simplest and most fundamental ways to show respect. We demand apologies from our children, but all too often we don't produce them ourselves.

It is as though we think that by saying "sorry" or admitting a mistake we will somehow undermine our parental authority or confuse our children about who is in charge.

Actually, quite the contrary is true. If we never apologize to our kids, it is as though we think we are infallible and want our kids to think the same. That sets us up as hypocrites without humility and undermines our children's respect for us.

When you make a mistake, even one as small as losing your temper a little or blaming a child for something he didn't do, make a full apology, including asking his forgiveness. If the mood and the opportunity is right, turn it into a mini-discussion about how everyone makes mistakes and how admitting them and saying we are sorry allows us to grow and to be less likely to make them again. It also is a way of saying "I love you" and "I respect you."

Feeling Spiritual Respect for a Kid Who Is Driving You Crazy

Let's face it. Along with the joy that comes with parenting come days that are exhausting, exasperating, sometimes almost debilitating! Sometimes our children can drive us to distraction! A frazzled young mother at her wit's end while she was running errands with two pre-schoolers screaming and fighting in the backseat, swooped into a drive-through and a voice coming from the microphone asked, "Can I help you?"

She quickly ordered some hamburgers and fries, thinking that maybe it would "calm the savage beasts."

After a few moments of silence the voice on the other end said, "Ma'am . . . do you realize that you're at the drive-in window of the bank?"

At a www.powerofmoms.com motherhood retreat, I found myself

sympathizing with a mother who said, "I have a six-year-old who is driving me crazy! She disagrees with everything I say! If I say 'the sky is blue,' she says, 'No, it's NOT!' If I say, 'Didn't you think that was a great movie?' she says, 'I thought it was dumb!' She just loves to disagree with everything that comes out of my mouth! I often find myself in a full-on argument with a disagreeable six-year-old. Of course I love her dearly, but she is driving me crazy! How can I change her?"

"The one you need to change," I told her, "is yourself." The key to doing that, we decided together, is to put it all into a spiritual perspective. The good news is that we remember that her daughter is a beautiful child of God who is exploring her "universe" with her mom. The bad news is that she knows how to push her mom's buttons and get the reaction she wants (a confrontation that brings attention totally focused on her).

Having had the same "you're driving me crazy" thought with several of my own children a multitude of times, I found that I had to be prepared for the button-pushers and have a predetermined routine to get myself above the fray. If there was a legitimate concern, I would ask myself why the child might be doing this, then say a brief silent prayer, then try to listen even harder and then respond calmly—and that was usually the end of it. If the child's point was frivolous, I would simply distract him to get past the craziness.

Finally, include your family quest for respect in your family prayers. Ask for the Spirit to prompt you to remember who each person is and where you all came from and thus to treat one another as brothers and sisters.

Putting the Puzzle Together: Knowing More about Your Kids as Individuals

Along with respecting our children, we need to relentlessly pursue the challenge of knowing more about who they are, about what gifts they brought here with them, about what motivates them, about what makes them unique, both pro and con, and to seek insights about why God might have chosen to send them to *us!*

Much of this is done through observation, through thought, and through prayer. And when a parent is really trying, it seems that the real Parent rewards him or her with little flashes of insight, little epiphanies that make us smile and say, "Oh, yes, that's who he is!"

Here are two exercises that might help.

The "Five-Facet Review"

We don't have a crystal ball that will reveal to us every aspect of who our children are and what they can be, but we do have access to inspiration and guidance about what they need and about how they are doing in the various facets of their lives.

But, as mentioned, the inspiration and insights don't come without some work, thought, and prayer. Like so many things of the Spirit, it all depends on our spiritual initiative.

The best way we have found to make this happen is a regular, scheduled, "five-facet review." All this means is to set aside one evening a month to go to dinner someplace—have a date—and talk exclusively about your children. If you are a single parent, do it with one of your kids' grandparents or someone else who loves your children. If you have a blended family, this will be an invaluable exercise as you listen to what the genetic parent knows and what the "new parent" perceives about each child. Go through the five facets of each of your kids: physical, mental, social, emotional, and spiritual.

Here is a brief example of how the conversation may go: *"How is Brandon doing physically?"* Talk through any issues—from weight to teeth or eyes. How about exercise, sports, activity level—any health problems? If there is an issue, focus in on it, brainstorm about it. If it's all good, move on. *"How is he doing mentally?"* Talk about school, about how he learns, where his mental gifts are. Take notes about concerns and about what you intend to do about them (and about *who* will do it.)

"How is he doing socially?" Discuss friends, how he interacts, isolate areas that need attention. *"How is he doing emotionally?"* Danger signs? How does he handle things? Moody? What upsets him? And finally, *"How is he doing spiritually?* How is his heart, how is his faith, where is he doing well and where does he need help?

Take notes, think together. When you discover and isolate a concern, decide who will do what about it, knowing you will revisit it in your next five-facet review in a month. It is amazing, once you have focused in on something, how ideas and solutions will come to you. Give each other assignments (for example, Mom to Dad: "Can you read with David twice a week this month? You'll see that he isn't on grade level with his reading skills.")

You know more than you think you do, and your spouse knows more than you think he or she does about each child! It just takes a discussion and some questions to pull out things you didn't even know you knew.

Pray before and after. Ask for guidance from the true Parent. Seek insights about the needs and the worries but also about the gifts and potential of your child.

You know more than you think you do, and your spouse knows more than you think he or she does about each child! It just takes a discussion and some questions to pull out things you didn't even know you knew.

You will come up with specific things to work on each month, and they will be your own thoughts. The things you think of and the inspiration you receive will be much more useful (and much more specifically geared to your child) than anything you will ever find in a parenting book (including this one!).

Keeping a "Personal Book" about Each Child

One of the most enjoyable and gratifying things that I have ever done for my children as their mother has also been one of the most useful in terms of coming to better know who each of them really is.

I had heard moms, including my own, say things like, "That's so cute. I better write that down so I can remember it." I wanted to keep a "mother's journal" and at some point I got the idea to make it like an ongoing letter to each of my children, something that I would one day give to them.

I decided when our first child was born to buy a journal and keep a record, first of the circumstances surrounding her birth and the joy of her "birth day!" I decided that I would then record things about her personality as she grew up. Cute things she said or did. "Dear Saren, you took your first step today and you were so proud of yourself. You tried it again and again even though each try ended up with a tumble. . . ."

I must admit that I was really good about doing this for the first few kids but as the demands got greater and life was filled with the normal chaos of having a big family, I found that I was months and sometimes even years behind in recording their lives.

However, about every six months or so I would decide on a day to "disappear" and catch up on their books. Sometimes I went to a motel room overnight, sometimes I just went to a shady spot in our old van for an afternoon and later I took some of the books on long airplane trips so I could catch up on my observations of each child. I recorded what had happened in their lives since the last writing and tried to decipher little notes I had thrown in the book about cute things they had said.

I now reflect on how terrific that process would have been if I'd had a computer or a blog where I could record what had happened in the life of each child at the end of each month . . . or six months or a year, depending on how diligent I was or how many kids I had at the time.

Yet there is something about the handwritten word that makes it a bit more meaningful.

When I had them, I put pictures in their books. Since a picture is worth a thousand words it cut down on the number of words I needed write. Even though it took some time and effort, the book was my gift to them on their wedding day.

In hindsight, I realized that what I had written probably did me more good than it did them! As I read through the entire book in the weeks before their weddings I was amazed at what I saw as the picture of their personalities up to that point. The most amazing thing was that the observations I had of them on the day they were born were almost a perfect description of them on the day they were married.

Their personality traits showed up again and again as I reread the story of their lives. I realized once more that "they are who they are!" Yes, as parents we provided some good soil, water, fertilizer, and sunshine to enable those little seedlings to grow. Yet what came through so loud and clear as I read through each of those books cover to cover just before each marriage was that those children were most certainly children of our Heavenly Father sent to earth to receive bodies and to be given a home where they could learn certain lessons. But those spirits placed in physical bodies were *still* who they were when they left that heavenly presence! Those were such wonderful "aha" moments when I saw things wholly that I wasn't able to see while I was "in the mire."

Helping Kids Know More about Their Spiritual Selves

It's not just about us knowing more about our kids, it's about helping them to know more about their own spiritual selves. Some of the ideas that follow may help you to do this or may prompt related ideas of your own.

"Remember Who You Are"

I used to think I was the only boy who had a mother who, every time I left the house, and I do mean *every* time, would yell at me, "Remember who you are!" I have since learned that it is quite a common parting shot among parents, including Teddy Roosevelt's mother.

It means a lot of good things, such as uphold the family name, make me proud, don't do anything stupid, be careful, think, etc. But have you thought what it means in the eternal context? Remember who you really are: a child of God, a spiritual being having a mortal experience, a person who has taken upon himself the name of Christ, a priesthood holder, etc.

And we want our children to remember those things not just so they will behave better, but so they will feel more self-worth, treat their bodies with respect, make good choices, be kind to others, and protect themselves and their standards. We could give them continual lectures on all these points, but maybe the best way to say it really is, "Remember who you are."

But to maximize the meaning of that admonition, we have to talk about it. Find ways to communicate with your children about who they are spiritually. A family home evening would be a perfect forum for this.

One good way to get that message across is a game that can be played with almost any age. It's played by simply making a list of every correct answer you can think of to the question "Who are you?" A player can start with his name, and can say things like "a sixth grader" or "a swimmer," but as the list builds, the most important answers, the spiritual ones, will make their appearance. The second step in the game is to circle the spiritual answers, which will lead to some kind of a discussion of them, especially if you ask the right questions, such as, "How many people on the earth know that answer?" "How important is that answer?" "How does knowing that make you feel about yourself?"

Decisions in Advance

We all know that it is good to let kids make choices, and from an early age. "What color of juice do you want, green or orange?" And simple choices also make behavior modification easier and avoid power struggles: "Do you want a lot of spinach or a little?"

As children get older, of course, choices become more important, and decisions get more difficult. When they make a bad choice, it is usually because they are not prepared for the situation they find themselves in. The best discussion and exercise we know on choices can be part of a process that is incorporated into the following idea.

Give your child a special journal inscribed with his or her name. A birthday is a good time to start this and to make it memorable. For some, eight may be a perfect age to begin the process that will follow. Other kids will internalize it better at ten or twelve. Sit down with your child one-on-one when you present him with the journal and ask him to turn to the last page and write this title at the top:

Decisions I Have Made in Advance

Then explain that this is a special book where he will record things he has decided to do for the rest of his life.

Start with a fun interchange that involves things your child can decide right now as opposed to things that he'll have to wait until later to decide. It might go something like this: "James, can you decide right now who you're going to marry?" James will normally be horrified and exclaim that he'll have to wait much longer to know that! Then ask if he can decide right now how many kids he'll have, where he'll live in ten years, or what kind of car he'll drive in fifteen years.

After you've established that there are lots of things you can't decide right now, go on:

"When you've really decided in your own mind and are going to promise yourself that you're going to do something or not do something, we want you to write it down and sign it. You should also write the date so you can remember the exact day you made the decision. This is entirely your choice. We don't want you to write anything just because you think Dad and I want you to write it. It has to be your own decision."

"Let me give you an example: Can you decide right now that you're never going to take drugs?"

Let's say that James jumps at the chance to say, "Yes, of course I can. I will never take drugs! Let me write that down. I'm sure of that!"

That is when you make James think, by making up a little scenario: "James, you may think that it will be easy never to try drugs right now, but that decision may be harder than you think when you actually face it. You are ten now, but in six more years you'll be sixteen. What

> **Common Decisions in Advance**
> - I will never cheat on tests.
> - I will not participate in pornography in any form.
> - I will be married in the temple.
> - I will not smoke, drink, do drugs (they may want to list these separately).
> - I will stay morally clean (some of our children listed specific ways they intended to keep this promise to themselves).
> - I will get a college degree.
> - I will continue piano lessons until I finish high school.
> - I will pay a full tithe.
> - I will go on a mission.
> - I will keep my body in shape and follow the positive food advice in the Word of Wisdom.
> - I will accept all Church callings.

if a girl that you *really* like at school asks you to come to a Saturday night party with her friends? This girl is one of the most popular in the school and you tell her that you'd love to come.

"When you get to the party you are even more excited because, by the kids you see there, you know you are about to become part of the in-crowd at school. After about half an hour, this girl comes to you and opens her hand to show you a little white pill. She says, 'James, you are about to have an amazing experience. Just swallow this pill and awesome things will happen. It's not really like an addictive drug. You'll feel the same as you do now by the time you go home.' Everyone is clustered around, watching you.

"What would you say, James?" If he is puzzled and unsure, tell him that he is probably not ready to write down that decision in advance just yet. Tell him you will give him some more situations later and he can think about it a little more.

On the other hand, James might be strong and resolved about it and say something such as, "I would say, I promised myself when I was ten years old that I would never take drugs! Do you want me to break my promise?"

Then you say, "Right on, James!" That boy has already thought about what might happen and is ready with an answer. He has made a decision and he is ready to write it on that first page of his journal, date it, and sign it.

Written "decisions in advance" are not a guarantee, but they are another deterrent and a further safeguard for your children so they don't get blindsided into making quick, foolish decisions that can devastate their lives and yours.

We have taught this principle to countless families across the world and have been amazed not only at the warm reception to the idea but also at the great things that parents and kids have come up with to decide in advance.

Most parents who have started and stuck with this idea—letting children add to their lists, decision by decision, but always after a thorough discussion with some future-oriented situations—have found that some great decisions can be made at very early ages.

Help your children make each decision a matter of prayer. Pray with your child about what decisions to make in advance. Once they are made, include them in your prayers. Encourage children to pray for the strength and the Spirit's guidance that they will be able to always live by the decisions they have made.

The "Second Seventh"

About the time a child reaches adolescence or becomes a teenager, the decisions-in-advance discussion can be taken to a new level. We like a discussion with eight- to fourteen-year-olds that builds around these questions from a parent:

- Do you know what the life expectancy is for someone your age? (About eighty-five years.)
- If you were to divide an eighty-five-year life into sevenths, how long would each seventh be? (About twelve years.)
- So which seventh of life are you in right now? (The start of the second seventh.)
- Do you think your second seventh, the one you're going into now, is a pretty important seventh?
- What are some of the decisions you will probably make during that second seventh or very early in the third seventh? (College, mission, marriage, children, where to live, kind of friends, tithing, attending Church, being honest, Word of Wisdom issues, etc.)
- How important are those decisions?
- Will they affect your life and your happiness in the other five sevenths?
- Does it seem fair that you have to make most of them in that second seventh, while you are so young?
- Can you make some of them in advance? Like right now? Which

43

ones? (The ones based on right and wrong, usually the ones with only two alternatives.)

• How about the others? (Since they have many alternatives and we don't know what they all are yet, we have to wait to make them.)

• How do we make them when we think we have the alternatives? (By studying them out in our minds and praying for confirmation as outlined in the ninth section of the Doctrine and Covenants.)

Children can learn this pattern at a surprisingly young age. Our daughter, Saren, who was in a British school while we served our mission in London, found herself slightly ahead of one class and slightly behind the next class. We were given a choice between moving her ahead to a stern taskmaster of a teacher named Mrs. Keebler or allowing her to remain another year with a teacher named Miss Christie, whom she dearly loved.

We gave the choice to Saren and tried to help her make it properly. She listed the pros and cons of each option. She thought about it and we talked about it. She came close to making the comfortable choice of staying with Miss Christie, but did not feel good about it as she prayed. She finally decided on the more challenging alternative of moving into a grade with slightly older kids where she would be a little behind and have to deal with Mrs. Keebler. She felt good about it as she prayed and it was her decision.

She had some tough times that next year, and we knew that if we had made the choice for her, she would have blamed us. As it was, she had the courage of her confirmation and she fought through the adjustments and finally, by the end of the year, felt good about her decision.

God, of course, could make choices for us, but then this life would promote increasing dependence and God-blaming rather than growing independence and gaining qualities like God.

A Lesson on Decisions from a Prophet

I was fortunate to learn an unforgettable (and very personally taught) lesson from a prophet after my return from my mission. It was a long time ago, but let me tell that story as best I can remember it, because it illustrates a principle we should all teach our children.

I had come home from my mission and been back in school for over a year when I fell head over heels in love. I was so goofy in love that I was not even able to think coherently. I couldn't sleep, I couldn't eat, I couldn't think about anything else.

And I was scared to death. One drawback in believing in eternal marriage is that it makes the decision huge! How could one so young and foolish as I make an eternal decision?

One sleepless, lovesick night I remembered something that gave me a flash of hope and of courage. During my mission I had driven Elder Harold B. Lee (of the Council of the Twelve and later to become the prophet) around to his appointments, and when the day was over he had thanked me and said, "If I can ever be of help after you come home, come and see me."

I didn't stop to think that he probably said that to every missionary he met. In fact I didn't stop to think about anything. I just got up from my bed in Logan at six in the morning and drove to Salt Lake to take him up on his offer. I got to the Church Administration Building before it had even opened.

With brain barely functioning, I waited until it opened and then marched up to Elder Lee's office. He had kind of a gruff secretary who took my name and who I think was probably useful in keeping people like me away. I blurted out, "I need to see Elder Lee."

"So do a lot of people, young man. Did you have an appointment?"

"No, but I *really* need to see him."

Something in my tone must have impressed her (maybe I sounded suicidal), and she went back into his office, returning with something like, "He's waiting for an appointment but you can go in for a minute."

Elder Lee stood and greeted me by name, and my deranged mind thought, "Ahhh, he remembers me," forgetting that I had given the secretary my name.

"Sit down, Elder Eyre, what can I do for you?"

"Well," I stammered, "I need to know if I should get married."

"Easy," he said with a broad smile. "You should!"

"No, no, I mean, should I get married to this certain girl."

"Oh, well now, that's a little harder. Tell me about her. Can she bake a cherry pie?" He was having fun now. I had become his comic relief. But to my tied-in-knots psyche he sounded serious, and I actually tried to answer the question.

"Ah, well, I'm not sure . . . but she gave me a cookie she baked the other day."

At this point, either because he saw that my condition was rather serious or maybe because his appointment was coming, he got down to business. He said, "Do you know how to make this kind of big decision?" And without waiting for my answer, he thumbed through his big triple combination scriptures, then turned the book around and slid it across his desk to me. "Read the verses marked there in the ninth section."

I remember thinking, *He knows!* I had been reading, over and over, that ninth section because I knew it was the formula. *How did he know?* The problem was that I had studied it out and studied it out. Heaven knew, I had thought of nothing else for days! Yet I had had no burning in my bosom, no answer, no sure feeling!

I thought, *Maybe this is a special Apostle's edition with extra stuff in it!* Yet I read the verses and felt almost disappointed that they said the same as mine.

"But that's what I've done, Elder Lee, that's all I have done. I've asked and asked if it is right, and I still don't know."

"If what's right, Elder? What have you asked is right?"

"Well, if Linda is right."

I remember the big smile that came to his face, as he shared what he had just figured out about me and gave me the answer. "It's not about Linda, or about you. What you must ask is if your decision is right! You have left out the middle step. First you study and pray and think, then you make the best decision you can, and then you ask God to confirm your decision. He put you here with agency. He will confirm your decision but He will not make the decision for you."

> *We don't get an owner's manual at the hospital with a new baby, and kids don't come with an instruction book or with a spiritual history that tells us the details of who they were in the premortal life.*

He put his arm around my shoulders and led me to the door, starting to have a little fun again. "Elder," he said, "I have the feeling that you have already made your decision. I can see it in your eyes. Think it through one more time though, be sure it is your decision, and then fast for at least a day and take your decision to the Lord in earnest prayer. It's your decision you pray about. Ask for confirmation. I promise you that you will then get either a confirmation or a stupor of thought."

It led to one of the most spiritual experiences of my life, and to the best and most important decision I have ever made.

Making the Most of Patriarchal Blessings

We don't get an owner's manual at the hospital with a new baby, and kids don't come with an instruction book or with a spiritual history that tells us the details of who they were in the premortal life. But we can come pretty close to getting that last one a few years later, when our kids receive their patriarchal blessings.

Can you imagine anything more marvelous than the voice of the Lord, through an ordained patriarch, telling your child (and you) of her spiritual lineage, of his foreordinations, of the gifts to be developed here, and the blessings that await?

As with anything that is somewhat expected, somewhat standard or usual, we may have a tendency to take patriarchal blessings for granted, or at least not to make as big a deal of them as we could or should.

How about this: If you have children who have yet to have their patriarchal blessings, build it up in advance. Devote family home evenings and private talks to what a blessing is, what it might contain, how it can be a help and a guide in future life to decisions, and what to watch for and pray for.

After the blessing (or with any child who has already had one), help create beautiful, permanent, easy-to-access copies (either physical, laminated ones or electronic ones that can be accessed online or on their phone). Talk about the blessings whenever opportunities arise. Ask questions such as, "Do you see anything in there that might give you a clue to what you should study in college? Or what you should do professionally? Or the kind of person you will marry? Or to what kind of temptations you have to watch out for?"

We had one child who took her blessing so seriously that she memorized it. She would quote little parts from it in situations where they applied, and it impressed some of our other kids so much that they memorized theirs too, and even finally shamed me into memorizing mine. As many times as I had read it, something about committing it to memory gave me additional insights and connections as a father that I am still grateful for. It's as though the memorizing put things onto my mental hard drive in a way that allowed the needs or situations I faced to access an exact phrase or portion at exactly the time it was most relevant. The memorizing gave me real-time recall of personal prophecies that were my greatest and deepest insights as to who I was and who I could be.

As a mother, I have loved hearing our children receive their blessings. The spirit in our children's blessings was so strong that if I closed my eyes, I could almost feel that father Abraham was standing right there by us!

An insightful friend suggested at one time that most patriarchal blessings contain challenges and promises. Recording those challenges on one side of a piece of paper and the promises on the other is a good way to inventory both and to begin to see and access ways to do better at tackling the challenges so that the promises will be fulfilled.

In addition to being sure our children have nice copies of their blessings, it is also important for us

> *Children who view themselves not just as kids but as beings who lived with God and who stood with God as loyal supporters for His plan of mortality and agency will have more confidence, more perspective, and more resistance and resilience with regard to the hard knocks of growing up in this world.*

parents to have copies close at hand. I have a copy of each of our children's blessings, and it gives me great comfort to read them, especially when they are going through turbulent times.

Really Teach about the Premortal Existence

Sometimes the best methods are the most direct ones. The more our children understand and think about the premortal life, the more aware they will be of their spiritual natures and of the paradigm that they are "spiritual beings having a physical experience."

Children who think of themselves in this way, who view themselves not just as kids but as beings who lived with God and who stood with God as loyal supporters for His plan of mortality and agency will have more confidence, more perspective, and more resistance and resilience with regard to the hard knocks of growing up in this world.

Make the premortal life an important and recurring part of your conversations. Ask questions such as, "Do you think you knew you would have that experience before you came here?" Or, "You're sure good at that. Do you think you developed that gift back in the premortal existence?"

Remind your children that they must have been choice and noble spirits in the pre-earth life, because they were reserved to come to the earth in these latter times and to have the restored gospel. Help them keep the earthly worries and frustrations and insecurities they face in perspective by putting them in an eternal context.

IMPACTS

As you keep yourself reminded of the first spiritual solution of remembering who your children really are and where they came from, and as you help *them* to appreciate their spiritual identity, it will make a positive difference both in the good things you can bring to pass and in the bad things it will help them avoid or overcome.

What Remembering Our Children's Spiritual Identity Helps Us Bring to Pass

More respect. Just remembering their eternal spiritual identities will channel additional respect from you to your children and from them to you.

More self-worth. The more our children are aware of their glorious, even royal premortal existence, the less they will be affected by momentary failures, by gender confusion, or by peer-group criticism or shunning.

Better friends. Aware of their eternal nature, they will try harder to be with those who share their values (and to influence those that don't more than they are influenced by them).

More appreciation and development of talents. Knowing that talents are God-given and eternally valued makes your children value them more.

A greater tendency to take care of their mortal body. If kids grasp why they have been given a physical body, they will be more likely to eat right, stay fit, care about safety, and avoid eating disorders and sexual abuse.

Good choices. Remembering where they came from will give your children an enhanced motivation for good decisions and a better sense of long-term consequences.

A greater desire to learn. Knowing the purposes of mortality will result in better grades and a tendency for your children to apply themselves more at school and in other activities.

What It Helps Children Avoid or Overcome

Peer Pressure. Doing what God wants emerges as more important than what friends say or think.

Bullying. Your child will be less likely to bully others and will be more capable of handling it if it happens to him.

Bad-influence friends. The feeling of knowing who they are makes children secure enough to influence more than be influenced.

Rudeness and disrespect. Understanding our relationship to God makes everyone love each other more and disrespect each other less.

Sibling rivalry and jealousy. Grasping that we each have unique gifts and that God loves us all equally makes children less resentful and competitive with others in the family.

Feeling left out or insecure. Thinking of oneself as an eternal child of God makes cliques and belonging to a group seem less important.

Acting out. From drugs to pornography and sexual experimentation, a higher opinion of oneself makes kids less attracted to aberrant behavior and less tempted.

SOLUTION

2

Remember God's Parenting Patterns

Follow the supreme example of how God parents us. *There has only ever been one perfect Parent, and the more we can learn of and emulate Him, the better parents we will be.*

The conversation started simply enough . . .

"Can you believe Samantha turns eight this summer? You'll be baptizing her!"

"Amazing! Where does the time go? It seems like she should still be about four!"

"You know, I've been thinking, since she's the third child, she gets lost in the shuffle so much. We should make a really big deal of her baptism."

Kate and Dave were enjoying a rare moment alone as they drove the fifty miles back from a wedding reception in the next town, and their conversation had turned to their kids.

"It's interesting, even though I still think of Sam as a little girl, I notice every once in a while how fast she is growing up—too fast! and she was asking me the other day if she could have a cell phone!"

"She thinks she should get everything Trace has, even though he's four years older."

"Yeah, and Trace thinks he should have everything Liz and her eighth-grade friends have."

"Have you noticed that we try so hard to be fair and to treat them all the same that we forget how different they are? Not only different in age, but different in every way—different needs, different motivations— it's like what we really need is a whole new formula for each of them."

"Oh, please! Who's going to figure all that out?"

Both Dave and Kate knew that this discussion was long overdue. Liz, at fourteen, was showing some classic signs of rebellion. Trace, about to become a deacon, was lazy and unmotivated. Samantha, whose up-coming baptism had started the conversation, seemed to think she was entitled to have whatever she wanted, without any effort, and right now! And little Mark, only three, seemed to be relishing (and prolonging) his time as the baby of the family, refusing to do anything for himself and expecting everyone else in the family to wait on him hand and foot.

They had prayed hard about their kids the night before and now, in the peaceful moments as they drove along together, ideas began to come.

"Let's make a big deal of Sam's baptism, Kate, not only because she needs attention, but because it is a big deal! Let's make it a real rite of passage and kind of promote her to middle management in the family. She needs some responsibility. She is really good with little Mark, and she needs more specific assignments around the house."

"And (gulp), maybe it's time to have the sex talk with her. She hears more than we know, and from the worst sources—media and friends."

"Age eight really is key, when you think about it. It's so transitional. She's old enough to really get things, but she's not cynical yet like Trace, or rebellious like Liz. You know, when you think about it, she's really flattered by being given responsibility right now."

"It's true! And most amazing of all, she still thinks we know something! That's not going to last long! It's like a little window of time before we have another teenager to deal with. I think we should take this age of accountability thing really seriously!"

"I'm into that whole 'rite of passage' thought. Let's tell her how important we think age eight and baptism and receiving the gift of the Holy Ghost is and make her feel special about it, including giving her some extra responsibility. And let's make a big deal about telling her some things that will make her feel trusted and accountable."

> *While other religions may call God "Father" as a term of respect or as a way of subjugating themselves to Him, we have a very different reason and a much more literal meaning when we say "Heavenly Father."*

The discussion went on between Dave and Kate (and it wasn't all quite as "aha, how wonderful" as we portrayed it here), but it was one of those lovely, Spirit-guided discussions that prayerful parents sometimes have when inspiration comes and when breakthroughs are made in how we think about our children within our unique eternal perspective.

Let's have that same kind of discussion between writer and reader in this chapter as we focus on the marvelous advantage of knowing a substantial amount about how God parents us!

INSIGHTS

More Than a Term of Respect

While other religions may call God "Father" as a term of respect or as a way of subjugating themselves to Him, we have a very different reason and a much more literal meaning when we say "Heavenly Father."

We mean it exactly literally. He is the Father of our spirits. We were born as His spirit children and lived in His family before this world was.

And what a treasure of parenting truth we have as we look at how our Heavenly Father has parented us and continues to parents us!

And isn't it a natural tendency to follow the patterns of our own parents?

"I Am Becoming My Mother"

One young mother actually made a list of the things that her mother had done with her that she would NEVER do with her own children.

Then one day when she was at her wit's end with the bickering and arguing of two of her children, she happened to catch a glimpse of her own reflection in a mirror as she was yelling at and lecturing her kids about not hurting each other.

The sound of her own voice and the sight of her own reflection was so exactly like how she remembered her own mother that she gasped, stopped in midsentence, and walked from the room thinking, "I am becoming my mother!"

We have all had similar experiences. Perhaps not that dramatic or negative, but we all find ourselves unconsciously, subconsciously, or consciously imitating our own parents.

One of the real tragedies in the world is that bad parenting and the abuse and belittlement of children passes down from one generation of parents to the next. Scripture hints at that when it says that the sins of the fathers are visited on the children for generations and depicts how the "traditions of their fathers" (Mosiah 1:5) can drag families down for hundreds of years.

There are areas of the world that are still developing where we love to go for many reasons and yet, at the same time, we hate to go there because in these areas it is a common, accepted part of their culture to hit children. It is the only form of discipline they know and the standard way to show disapproval. In other cultures, excessive entitlement and leniency are problems of an opposite nature.

The fact is, most parents perform their parenting pretty much like their parents did, and thus a parent who changes and turns away from the bad methods and child-damaging patterns of many generations is a true hero and may start a new and better parenting pattern that will flow down through his posterity.

Following the Heavenly Parent Rather Than the Earthly One

Wouldn't it be wonderful if the patterns we pick up and the methods and examples of parenting that we follow could be those of our Heavenly Father? If we can emulate how He raises us we will become the best parents we can be and it will cause our children to be the best—and the happiest—that they can be.

So the second spiritual solution is remembering and thinking about and following the divine example! If we can explore everything we know about His pattern of parenting, then we can attempt to apply each of His ways to how we parent our (His) children.

> ❧
>
> *Follow the divine example! Explore everything we know about His pattern of parenting and then attempt to apply each of His ways to how we parent our (His) children.*
>
> ❧

Of course, none of us will measure up to the perfection of God's parenting, and you may wonder if we should even make the comparison. It can be daunting, even discouraging, to try to follow a perfect model.

But here's the thing: When we try, He will help! Any time we look to a mentor or model ourselves after someone we admire, that mentor does what he can to help us. How true this can be in the ultimate situation, when we view God Himself as our ideal and work consciously to know and to follow His wise and complete example. Perhaps when we are earnestly trying and yet still fall short, He will lift us up and pull us along toward Him.

So here is a list of some of the things we know about how God, our Heavenly Father, parents us. We will number them so they will match up with the "applications" to follow—with the efforts we can make to apply them in our own parenting. We have come up with fifteen of them—some may just be insights to enjoy, and others will beg for more attention from you as you consider how you raise your own children. And you'll have additional ideas and applications of your own.

1. God grants us complete, unconditional love. Talk about starting with the obvious (and perhaps the hardest one to follow!).

We know that God has a deep and unconditional love for each of us and that His love is individual rather than collective. He loves the drug addicts, the sinners, and even those who revile him, even as He loves those who are true and faithful to His teachings. He knows and appreciates the uniqueness that each of us has, and He applies equal (and total) love in different ways (as many different ways as He has different children).

Heavenly Father and Jesus Christ not only show their love for us, they tell us of their love, in countless ways. They tell us through sunsets and wildflowers. They tell us through the random acts of kindness of those we encounter. They tell us through comfort in hard times and little miracles every day.

2. God sees (and treats) each child as a unique and eternal individual. Have you heard the parenting advice, "Be fair, treat all of your kids the same"? That's not Heavenly Father's method. He has lovingly put us each into a body, a situation, and a series of circumstances tailored to what each of us needs. He knows each of us perfectly and loves the uniqueness that makes us each who we are.

3. God gives clear, simple laws with well-announced consequences, rewards, and punishments. Our Heavenly Father has never been subtle or ambiguous about His rules. He wrote them in stone. He gave them to prophets. He wrote them in scripture, and He often states the reward or the punishment right with the law.

It is by having immutable laws that God gives us the boundaries in which He expects us to operate. He gives us agency, but He also makes clear His laws, along with the rewards for compliance and the penalties for deviance.

4. God allows His children the chance to repent. Heavenly Father doesn't want any of us to fail. His laws are not negotiable, and He knows we will fall short, so there is a provision for repentance. And with the repentance comes complete forgiveness.

> *It is by having immutable laws that God gives us the boundaries in which He expects us to operate. He gives us agency, but He also makes clear His laws.*

This is made possible, of course, by the Atonement of the Savior which allows God's children to overcome the sins that would otherwise prevent us from returning to Him.

5. God taught us and trained us and held us close throughout the premortal life, and then He gave us choices and let us go. God, in His marvelous model for parenting, held us close, kept us with Him in His home, and taught us all He could for eons. And then, when further progress required the responsibility, choice-making, independence, and families of our own that could not happen in His presence, He gave us our agency and let us go.

With agency came choices, and the decision-making started with a bang—with perhaps the biggest choice of all being whether we would follow what must have seemed an unbelievably risky plan of veiled mortality, temptation, options, and pain.

It was time for the irony of leaving our heavenly parents so we could become more like them. It was time to apply what we knew (but first having to remember it despite the veil) and to make our own decisions and set our own course.

6. God trusts His children and is completely trustworthy for His children. God trusts us mightily! And He *entrusts* us. He trusts us enough to send us into this dangerous mortality. He entrusts us not only with our own salvation but also with the stewardship of others of His spirit children.

And, of course, God is completely, totally, and endlessly trustworthy. What He says is what He does. He is His word, and He is The Word. His promises are always kept.

One form of trust is covenants. After turning us loose and putting us on our own, God seeks ways to bind us to Him, ways to help us remember who we are, even through the veil, and ways to pull us back toward Him once we start to drift. So He gives us covenants.

As we learn in Primary, a covenant is a two-way promise between us and the Lord. We pledge ourselves to do something righteous, and He promises blessings in return.

7. God gives us stewardships. Heavenly Father, who owns all in His universe, gives us stewardships. Our first stewardship is of our agency, followed by so much more, and He does so with the promise that we can someday *own* that which we learn to steward.

His stewardships are responsibilities, not entitlements.

8. God has a plan of happiness for His children. One of the most marvelous and awesome things that we know about God is that He has a magnificent and comprehensive plan for the ultimate happiness of His children.

We sometimes call it the plan of salvation. He has spelled it out for us in the restored gospel. He has told us that the purpose of mortality is joy. He has explained to us that trials, sorrow, and opposition are as much a part of it as happiness and fulfillment. And He has made it clear that His plan, and our eternal progress, centers around families.

9. God gives us written advice in the form of scripture. Heavenly Father knows and values the written word, as do His prophets. Lehi sent his boys back, at the peril of their lives, to get written records. The full word of our Heavenly Father is written in His scriptures. Language and writing lend clarity and permanence to the laws and wisdom of God.

10. God allows us constant availability to Him through prayer and suggests regular communication. With God, there are certain set times when we anticipate spiritual communication—when we partake of the sacrament, when we kneel in family prayer, when we have our personal bedtime prayers. These are like set appointments for spiritual meetings that keep us in tune and in touch. Yet we don't need an appointment to converse. We can "call" anytime, and the line is never busy, nor is our Father ever unavailable.

11. God sent His eldest son to help and save us. Perhaps the most beautiful of all divine parenting stories involves the eldest son—a Father sending His Beloved Son to do something that only He could do for all of His younger brothers and sisters.

12. God sends angels. Far from leaving us on our own, Heavenly Father prompts and guides us through the Holy Ghost and also sometimes sends actual heavenly beings or angels to help us in times of special need.

13. God finds joy in His children and in His relationship with them. God's "glory" is the progress and eternal lives of His children, and "joy" is the purpose for which He made mortality. We know that He takes joy in our progress, in our learning, and in His individual relationship with each of us.

14. God gives us specific opportunities for service. Through His

Church, God gives us constant opportunities for service—service in the ward, service on missions, and compassionate service of all kinds.

He knows that our happiness, as well as the welfare of our fellow travelers in mortality, can be increased and enhanced by service.

15. God makes family central to all and the core of His purpose. Finally, as we think through what we know about God as a parent, we come to this: Heavenly Father's family is His priority, His "end" to which all else is the "means." His goal is to "bring to pass the immortality and eternal life" of His children (Moses 1:39).

APPLICATIONS

Now comes the challenge of looking at Heavenly Father's parenting pattern and asking ourselves how we can emulate each part of it.

1. Try to follow God's example of complete, unconditional love. Anytime we use words like "complete" and "unconditional" we are talking about perfection. And we can never reach God's perfection. But how do we begin to try?

Of course it involves the efforts discussed in the first solution—trying to understand who each of our children really is, and to discover each one's gifts, needs, and particular traits.

> *Heavenly Father's family is His priority, His "end" to which all else is the "means."*

Hard and complicated as that part might sound, there is another part that is shockingly simple. It's the tag line from the Church's classic "Homefront" media spots—and it's only six words: "If you love them, tell them!"

Heavenly Father and Christ not only show their love for us, they *tell* us of their love, in countless ways.

It is not enough to assume that our children know we love them.

When we just assume, we are a little like Alf from the old country, whose wife, Anna, used to plead, "You never tell me you love me!"

Alf would reply, "Anna, I told you that on the day we were married. If anything ever changes, you'll be the first to know!"

Instead, we should be like the father I used to home teach in Virginia years ago. He was kind of a rough fellow—a plumber by trade—and actually a man of few words. But his kids always seemed remarkably happy and well-adjusted, and they acted so secure and natural in his presence. As a young father I remember wondering how he did it. Years later, I ran into one of his daughters, then a student at BYU. I got reacquainted and then asked her what her dad's parenting secret was. She told me a remarkable thing. She said her father had a temper and was a little gruff at times, but that he did one thing that superseded everything else, and he did it every single night. She said he would tuck her in and then take her face in his rough hands and say, "Sweetheart, I love you. And you are more important to your mom and

How to express love on a daily basis

- Have special goodnight rituals of tucking kids in bed and saying prayers together (butterfly kisses, linking arms while kneeling, telling your "happy" and "sad" from the day, etc.).
- Analyze what each child's "love language" is. (Some kids need verbal praise, others appreciate little personal acts of service, some feel loved when a parent plays ball or does crafts with them.)
- Be there as often as you can to really talk with them when they get home from school. (A snack is a good motivator for them to want to sit and talk.)
- Say "I love you" at the end of each phone call and every time you say good-bye or part company during the day.

me than anything else. Don't you ever forget that." Then he would turn out the light and close her door.

Sometimes saying it more often makes us also show it more often, in more ways, to our kids. And it makes us think about them more and be aware of them more. *You can't overdo it!* There are lots of things we can give way too much of to our kids, but love is not one of them. They are sponges with an unlimited absorbing capacity for our honestly expressed and unconditional love.

Does unconditional love mean not correcting our children, not disciplining them? It certainly does not mean that to God who chastens those He loves (see D&C 95:1) and advises us to reprove at times with sharpness, but then show forth afterward an increase of love (see D&C 121:43). Love can mean giving critical feedback to our kids or using "tough love" when they require it.

Another phrase that parents can't repeat too often is, "I don't love what you just did, and there will be a consequence, but it does not change how much I love you." Even small children can understand that and can realize that our displeasure and discipline for something they have done does not diminish our love for them. Say it often enough, feel it, mean it, and show it, and they will begin to understand that your love is "undiminishable"—that it is unconditional.

2. See and think of each child as unique and eternal. This principle is a little counter to the idea that parents should be fair and treat each child the same. "But that's not fair!" One child will say when another gets off easier than he would have or gets some reward the first didn't get.

We have progressed in our answer over the years. We used to say, sometimes in exasperation, "Well, life's not fair!" Now we try to explain better. We ask, "What doesn't feel fair about this?" Then we explain, "We're trying to make sure that each of you gets what you really need and sometimes one of you will get more than someone else but other times it will be the other way around." Or, "Someday you will be a parent, and I hope when you are, you will try to give each of your kids exactly what they need and not the same thing you give the others."

Parents often tell us something such as, "Our older children are complaining incessantly that we don't treat their younger siblings as we did them. They are disgruntled that we are so much more lenient and we don't make them toe the line like we did with them." A friend once made the observation that no two kids ever had the same parents. What she meant, of course, is that we evolve as parents, and hopefully become better as we progress through life and through our kids.

As time evolves, things do change. As parents, we not only try to teach, we try to learn what works and what doesn't. We improve. We panic a little less. We are sometimes just too tired to make a mountain out of a molehill. We just keep doing the best we can and hope our kids will understand.

We will never know our children as well as God knows them (after all, He has been their parent—and ours—for eternity). But don't sell yourself short! You've known your ten-year-old for ten years and your sixteen-year-old for sixteen years, and you know a lot about him or her. Discover more and more about each child through thinking and praying and discussing (like in the five-facet review from the last chapter) and then give each child the kind of love he or she needs as a unique, one-of-a-kind spirit on whom only you and your spouse are the experts!

3. Establish clear laws, rewards, and punishments. Following God's pattern in the establishment of laws within our families can be beneficial on a number of levels.

Children who know their boundaries, even though they may complain about them, have a certain, simple security and identity that other kids don't feel. To be always pushing the envelope and not knowing what you can get away with is not a good feeling. And to know it will depend on the mood of your mom or dad at the moment makes everything kind of like a dangerous, moving target.

We like the word "law" more than "rule." "Law" seems to bother kids less and incite less mutiny than "rule." And it lends itself to better comparisons in teaching small children. "Why do we have traffic laws?" "Why do we have laws in our country that people have to obey?" Most important, God calls His commandments "laws" and we want our family laws to mirror His.

One huge benefit of clearly established and consistently followed family laws is that it allows parents to be more matter-of-fact about things. Have you noticed how the best moms and dads seem pretty calm most of the time—that they manage to avoid the emotion and drama and power struggle that plague so many parents? You hear them say (calmly) things such as, "Sorry, Matt, but that's the law," or "Don't blame me, you know that when the little hand is at the eight it's time to turn out the light," or "Thanks for telling me about your friend Tommy and what he gets to do, but in *our* family . . . ," or even, "I feel your pain, son, but that's what we agreed on."

We have had lots of fun establishing family laws through the years. When our first two daughters were three and two we started having family home evenings about family laws. We wanted them to be involved so we explained what a law was and then asked them what they thought would be a good family law. Our three-year-old's hand shot up and she said with confidence, "Never hit other little girls!"

"What a great idea!" we said as we saw the wheels in the mind of the two-year-old working.

"No pud in puds" (translation: "Never plug in plugs"), the two-year-old added as she remembered the lesson she had the night before when she tried to plug in a fork.

To make a long story short, we added to that list of family laws for years until one day our oldest, then eight, came to me and said, "Mom, we have thirty-three laws! We can't even remember all of them. In the whole Bible there are only Ten Commandments!"

We immediately realized that she was right! We needed to cut and simplify! In the end we all decided on five one-word family laws, each with a consequence attached to breaking that law.

Here are the Eyre Laws:

Peace

Respect

Asking

Order

Obedience

When we asked the kids to help us decide on what the consequence should be for breaking the law, they were hilarious. Assuming they would *never* break the law of *asking* (which meant always ask before they leave and always let us know where they are), they thought that the punishment should be being confined in their room for a whole day with only bread and water.

We decided that there should be a natural consequence for breaking each law. For example the consequence for breaking the law of *peace* was going to the Repenting Bench (more about that in a minute). The consequence for breaking the law of *respect* was simply to start over. (A parent who has heard something disrespectful from the mouth of a child should say, "Let's start over," until the child figures out how to say what he just said with more respect.) The consequence for leaving without *asking* was that the child was not allowed to go the next time he wanted to go to something. The consequence for breaking the law of *order* (leaving the play room messy or leaving their room in a mess) was that they couldn't play with or go with friends until it was clean. And the consequence for breaking the law of *obedience* was the magic word "please." (When we asked a child to do something, if we forgot to say please, there was no obligation to do what we asked, but if we said "please" there was no way out. They had to do it!)

Of course, this is not as easy as we are making it sound. Everything needed reinforcement over and over again in family home evening. We took one law at a time and really made sure that everyone knew exactly what was meant by that one-word law and what the consequence would be for breaking it. Role-playing various situations where one of the laws would apply was helpful.

We should take pains to make the setting up and maintaining of family laws a spiritual process. As you discuss and set up your family laws, pray about them as a family. Ask which laws would help your family be happier and please God most. Call on the children to pray about them. When they are set, pray together for the strength to keep them, and ask forgiveness for the times you have not.

4. Allow children the chance to repent. As well as we know God's provision for His children's repentance, we often fail to follow the same pattern in our own homes.

While the bigger problem may be the absence of family laws, how often we also see rigid, disciplinarian households where the letter of the law is so strictly enforced that there is no mercy. Even in homes that have done a good job setting up rules, there can often be too much "swift justice." "You break a law or make a mistake and you get immediate punishment so you won't do it again." That is a good policy if you are training a dog or a horse, but children deserve the same opportunity to repent that God gives us.

We finally figured that out many years ago while Richard served as mission president in London. We had four little kids when we arrived in England and six when we returned to the states three years later and— take it from me as a mother—the kids were a lot easier to count than the fights they had with each other. I was exhausted from playing judge, jury, and warden all day long. "Who started it?" "Then what did you do?" "Who hit the hardest?" It was nuts.

We realized one day that our home was a perfect microcosm for what happens in the process of repentance. We have been taught since the time we were small that repentance is a process: We break a law, we figure out what we did that wasn't in alignment with the Lord's will, we admit what we have done wrong and express our regrets, we make things right by asking for forgiveness from the person we have wronged, and then we promise to try not to do it again.

As we struggled with how we could make that process work with sibling rivalry, angry feelings, and even physical fighting, we came up with a solution called the Repenting Bench and it served us well for more than twenty years.

We went to a Church of England yard sale and bought a short, very uncomfortable-looking pew which was about three feet wide, just big enough for two children to sit together, uncomfortably.

We introduced the bench to the children in a family home evening and explained that this bench was now going to be placed in our kitchen and would henceforth be called "the Repenting Bench." We explained that whenever there was an argument or fighting between two children they would be sent directly to the bench where they would have to go through a process of repentance. First they must figure out what *they* did wrong (not what the other kid did). When they are ready to admit their fault, they must call Mom or Dad and say what they did. Then they must turn to the other person and say, "I'm sorry. Will you forgive me?" The other person then has to decide and, since they really want to get off the bench, they almost inevitably said, "Yes." The other child goes through the same process. Then they say, "I'll try not to do it again," give each other a little hug, and are allowed to leave the bench.

For most young children the repenting bench works like magic. The argument stops immediately. A stern "You two—to the repenting bench" will do it. You no longer have to be the referee or the arbitrator or the judge and deal out the punishment. Bad feelings between children are dissipated, and most important, children learn one of the most valuable things they came to earth to learn: the process of repentance!

That old bench has saved us countless hours of negotiation as we let the kids figure out how to resolve their own disputes. Constant arguments can build into resentments that may last a lifetime if they aren't resolved. Even though the process may seem perfunctory at times and kids will say, "Yes, I forgive you," just to get off the bench, it is undoubtedly the best thing we have ever found to reduce bad feelings between children and maintain a better spirit of love in our home. Somehow that physical hug at the end is like popping a bubble with your fingertip. Anger, angst, and even thoughts of revenge just disappear!

Incidentally, as empty nesters, we recently moved from our home of thirty years and decided to have a "family auction" of the furniture we didn't want to take with us. We gave each of our children ten thousand dollars in Monopoly money, hired a real auctioneer—complete with top hat, gavel, and fast-talk—and let each kid bid on the things he wanted. The most spirited bidding of the night was for—guess what?—the repenting bench. One of our sons (one of the feistiest ones) spent more than half of his bidding money to win the bench, and afterward, when I asked him why, he said, "Dad, I spent half of my life on that bench!"

Obviously, you don't need an old Church of England pew . . . any bench will work, or two chairs, or even a particular stair on your staircase—any close-proximity place that you designate as the repenting zone. It is important that it is always the same place, however, and it is crucial to role-play the whole thing over and over in a family home evening so that when you say, "Go to the repenting bench," there is no question about where to go and what to do.

By the way, it's likely that at least one of your kids will say something such as, "What about you! If you and Dad are arguing, can we send you to the bench?" The answer, of course, is *yes*. (We have spent many lovely moments "repenting" to each other under the watchful glare of one or more of our children.)

When repentance involves more than working out a conflict, it may require some extra one-on-one time between parent and child. At a recent family reunion, a young grandson scribbled through the pages of his girl cousin's journal. He thought it was funny and she was devastated! When asked point-blank, eyeball to eyeball, whether or not he did it, he firmly declared that he did *not*. Richard spent the next hour getting to the truth and unraveling the little web of lies the child had spun to deflect suspicion.

Once we got to the truth, there were tearful "I'm sorrys" and some genuine remorse. You could see the visible relief in that child's face as he felt the "lightness" that repentance brings after the dark feelings that he had harbored.

As children get older, it's important to help them understand the entire process of repentance, including asking for forgiveness from God, taking the sacrament meaningfully, seeking sanctification of the Holy Ghost, and so forth. But within the home, both older and younger children can learn and benefit from the repenting bench.

5. Teach and hold close, then let go. How do we emulate God's pattern of teaching and training His children and then letting them go? When does D-day come for our children? How early can we begin to give our children choices?

Perhaps in the premortal life there were stages that we progressed through in gradual and steady preparation for our agency and independence here on earth. The Church now gives us some guidelines and phases that may mirror this kind of step-by-step process of getting ready to leave home and parents. Small children go to nursery, where the simple goal is to play and cooperate and be entertained and taken care of (and occasionally learn some simple lessons.) They start going to

Primary classes at three and progress in terms of what they can understand. Then at eight comes the age of accountability with baptism and the gift of the Holy Ghost. At twelve, boys receive the priesthood and girls enter Young Women and both start serving within the ward. At sixteen comes further service along with driving and dating and other responsibilities which dovetail over the next few years into college and missions and marriage.

We have always tried to follow this pattern and age progression in terms of our parenting goals. Babies and toddlers are simply to be cherished and loved. At three or so, the goal is to give and enhance their capacities for joy. At eight, they are ready for (and flattered by) new levels of responsibility. At around twelve, the focus shifts to learning sensitivity and charity toward others. And about sixteen, there is more focus on the decisions and goal setting that will define their independent futures. Check out our website, www.valuesparenting.com, for more about these phases and their sequence.

Part of the challenge, as it must have been for God, is being aware of the different ages, levels, and needs of each of our individual children. Talking about their "five facets" (see p. 35) on a regular basis can help, and praying for insights and listening for answers is the best tool of all.

Generally, our children are ready for more choices and challenges than we think they are. But they need to start getting this independence in thoughtful and organized ways, not by just giving them free reign to do whatever they want. We have often made the statement to parents that, "In current western society, we give our children license too early and responsibility too late." We also like the one that says, "Wherever possible, retard your child's social growth."

In other words, phase in their independence, follow the guidelines of the Church, and treat them as your respected stewardships whom you want to help gradually grow to need you less and less.

And then, when it is time for them to leave for mission or schooling or marriage, really let them go rather than hovering and coddling and interfering.

6. Trust and be trustworthy / Give covenants. Can we follow God's pattern in trusting our children and allowing them to totally trust us?

And can we be trustworthy to God? Trust-worthy! Worthy of the magnificent trust He has given us. We know we are not worthy of His blessings. Are we worthy of His trust? Are we trustworthy?

As we strive to be trustworthy with God, it can lead us to be trustworthy with our children. We can absolutely pledge ourselves to do what we say we will do, and not to say that which we may not be able to do.

Can we make covenants with our children? Can we form pacts where we, in our best moments, promise each other things that will bind us and that will help to keep our children out of harm's way?

Here are a few illustrations of the kind of family pacts you could consider:

• **An honesty pact.** Discuss in family home evening how important it is to trust each other. Think of some case studies and role-plays. Get to a point where you each promise to all other family members to always tell the truth.

• **A respect pact.** Make a mutual pledge to speak with respect to family members and never to speak in a tone you would not use with a friend. Again, a family home evening is the best time to discuss and work on this.

• **A loyalty pact.** Promise to try to support each other in each person's interests and activities—to be there when someone is performing or competing and to try to choose family over friends when the two conflict.

• **A "no offense" pact (for grown children).** Adult children pledge to seek parents' advice whenever possible and not to be offended when it is given, and parents pledge not to be offended when adult children choose not to follow their advice.

7. Allow for stewardship. God, who owns all, gives us stewardships. Likewise, we parents, while owning everything in our households, can give our children stewardships, over things and over responsibility, with the promise and the hope that they will one day own all that we have and more.

We recommend using the word "stewardship" more with children, and talking a lot about what it means.

Consider getting rid of entitlement words like "allowance" and any practices you might have of giving kids whatever their friends have.

> *Create a "family economy" where everyone has certain responsibilities (for the common areas of the house, for the dishes, etc.) and where kids keep track of their stewardships.*

Instead, create a "family economy" where everyone has certain responsibilities (for the common areas of the house, for the dishes, etc.) and where kids keep track of their stewardships. Have a "payday" at the end of the week where how much they receive is based on how many of their responsibilities they remembered and got done. (For further details on this type of a family economy, go to www.valuesparenting/familyeconomy.com.)

8. Create a plan of happiness for your children. What is your plan for the happiness of your children?

A good place to start is with a family mission statement, where you and your children discuss, perhaps over several weeks and several family home evenings, what you want your family to be. Ask them, "What words describe our family?" "How should our family help us?" "What should we feel in our family?"

Begin to form a mission statement or slogan unique to your family.

Then ask yourselves as a couple (or, if you are a single parent, brainstorm with one of your parents), what your goals are for your children and how you think you can better facilitate their long-term happiness.

It is less important that you finish your plan than that you are working on one, and thinking about the goal of the long-term joy of your children.

9. Give written advice. How do we advise and guide our children? Will the occasional lecture or verbal instructions accomplish all we need and have the staying power we want? Or do we need to value the written word too?

Notes and letters (handwritten sometimes) of love and appreciation when our children do something especially kind or memorable or when they get their Young Women in Excellence Awards or their Eagle Scout awards will be treasures! And written bits of advice, carefully worded, can impact children long after what you may have said is forgotten.

Recorded and transcribed priesthood blessings, and other written records, have a permanence (and "reviewability") that verbal conversation or instruction does not. They are also better

How to use the written word

- Write Mother's Day or Father's Day notes to your children.
- Send special notes for big occasions.
- Keep your own journal to record your testimony for your children and posterity to read.
- Keep a journal with your kids where you write notes and advice to them and leave it on their beds. Then they write back and leave it on your bed.
- Show them your journals or letters from your mission or when you were younger so they can identify with how your testimony has grown and evolved.
- Keep a "children's journal"— essentially a long, ongoing letter to them—and give it to them on their wedding day.

thought out and usually better reasoned and composed than lectures, tongue lashings, or off-the-cuff advice.

10. Have regular communication times (and constant availability for calls). Can we try for a similar kind of in-touch-ness and availability with our children that God allows His children?

What it takes, first of all, is a priority commitment. We know one man, important and busy in his company, who instructs his secretary that calls she is to put through, no matter what, are the calls from his children.

Another friend has a "daddy date" with each of his children once a month where they have their dad all to themselves for an evening and they get to decide what the activity is.

Still another dad has a monthly "interview" with each of his kids on the second Sunday of each month.

One couple has a regular Sunday phone call to their grown kids.

A younger couple asks everyone to tell their "happies" and "sads" at the dinner table each evening.

One couple consciously applies "active listening" where they just repeat or paraphrase back what a kid says, without direction or correction or advice.

One mom has figured out that late at night is the time her teenagers will open up and talk. Another uses car time to get into conversations. Still another mom volunteers to drive car pools because kids "forget she is there" and talk about all kinds of things.

One mom told us that if she really wants her daughter to talk, she gives her a foot rub!

Whatever your personal formula, we need some set times for communication, and we need to find ways to make ourselves always available to our children and to get them to open up to us.

11. Allow older sons or daughters to help their younger siblings. Are there things that only our older children can do for our younger children?

Have you ever observed a big brother or big sister teaching a younger sibling something better than you could have taught it? Or have you watched how closely a younger child follows the example (good or bad) of an older brother or sister?

Active LDS families tend to be relatively large, and the more children you are dealing with, the greater your need for a little "middle management."

In our case, it started with homework. There were more kids than we could help, so we started assigning the older kids to help the younger ones. They liked it better when we called it "tutoring" so we began calling the older ones "tutors" and, before we knew it, the younger ones were getting referred to as "tutees." In general, those over eight and past the age of accountability were tutors and those under eight were tutees.

The tutees liked it right away! Who wouldn't rather have an idolized big brother or sister help them with their homework than a parent (particularly with their math!). And the more we praised the tutors (and thanked them and told them how much it was helping their tutees) the better they liked it too. We started having an occasional "tutors' night out" when we would have a babysitter come over for the little ones and take the tutors out for a reward in the form of a movie or dinner.

We're almost embarrassed to tell you how broadly the idea expanded. Before we knew it, we had tutors giving tutees their baths, getting them ready for Church on Sunday, cutting up their meat at the dinner table, telling them one-on-one bedtime stories, helping them brush their teeth, getting them ready for school, and putting them in bed after having their prayer with them. We even started having some family home evenings lessons just for tutors and then having them go and pass on the lesson information to their tutees.

And speaking of family home evenings, it seemed to work better when there was an official tutor-tutee designation—better than just asking one kid to help another kid on an ad-hoc basis. We would make the designations at the first family home evening of the month and change them if necessary at a subsequent FHE.

We would also have the tutees write detailed thank-you letters to their tutors, itemizing the things the tutor had helped them with.

12. Enlist the help of angels. You may read this subheading and wonder where this one is going. Surely one thing Heavenly Father can do that we could never imitate is that He can send angels to protect, to guide, and to help His children.

Is it possible that we, as parents, could do something even remotely similar to that?

Maybe there is something . . .

We all know that sometimes someone with a little "social distance" can reach one of our children better than we can. And our kids, sometimes just out of the politeness we have taught them or out of a little fear bred of unfamiliarity, will pay more attention to a nonparent than to a parent.

> *Who are your "angels"? Which of your friends will your children listen to? Which of your friends could convey a message or a warning or an idea that you are having a hard time relaying to a child?*

Who are your "angels"? Which of your friends will your children listen to? Which of your friends could convey a message or a warning or an idea that you are having a hard time relaying to a child?

Is this something we should be afraid to ask our friends to do? Is it an imposition or a big inconvenience? Often as not, it is something a friend would be glad to do, would actually enjoy doing it, and would be honored that you would ask.

Why not find our own angels in the form of our friends and ward members whom we can ask to give specific and particular advice and guidance to our children according to their needs.

13. Find joy in your kids and in your relationship with them. God makes "joy" the goal of our mortality. We should do the same for our children—and for ourselves. Parenting is not one continual joy! It is filled with hectic busyness, with worry, and with exhausting responsibility. We find ourselves wondering when we will have a rest! A friend of ours once changed the words of a wonderful song to make it more "realistic."

"There is beauty all around," he sings, "when there's no one home. Hate and envy ne'er annoy . . . making life a bliss complete . . . when there's no one home."

Despite the lack of peace and bliss that comes with children, there are also those great moments of joy. Moments when two kids play sweetly, when a child says the cutest thing, or gives a tender prayer, or lisps "I love you."

One mom has a "joy journal" where she simply writes a line or two whenever she has one of these moments. Another makes a short blog entry (often with a photo) to capture as many of them as she can.

They add up. And they help us get through the not-so-perfect moments that are an equal part of parenting.

14. Give kids more opportunities to serve and to give. One of the most interesting (and frequent) questions we get from parents all over the world is this: "How do I 'unspoil' my kids?"

There is certainly no quick fix for years of indulgence and entitlement, but one of the most effective and fast-acting antidotes we have found is to get a child more involved in organized service.

Ward cleanup projects may not be quite dramatic enough. Consider taking children to work in a soup kitchen or even possibly on a "service expedition" where, instead of a vacation some year, you go to a village in a developing country and work on a health, water, or nutrition project of some kind. There are many good, nonprofit organizations that put these together, offering surprisingly inexpensive "voluntourism" packages to villages in developing countries.

Kids come home noticeably changed from a week of sleeping on the ground in a village and working with villagers to build a well or a school or a clinic.

> *We are not some adjunct experiment to God or a sidelight of interest in an existence devoted to other things. We are His "work and [His] glory" (Moses 1:39).*

15. Acknowledge family as the center of all, as the core of our purpose. We are not some adjunct experiment to God or a sidelight of interest in an existence devoted to other things. We are His "work and [His] glory" (Moses 1:39).

Only as we are willing to think of our children in the same way—as our work and our glory—as our priority and our passion—only then will we draw down the full help and approval of Heavenly Father.

Some may get to this point in the book and say, "Where will I find the time to do all this stuff?" The answer is that this is not about borrowing a few minutes here and there or putting a little more thought into one of the many separate facets of your life. This is about adopting the same priority as God has and, in the process, working out your own salvation while you work on that of your children and your family.

IMPACTS

Of course, since God is the complete and perfect parent, emulating His parenting, if we could ever do it completely, would have a completely positive impact on every aspect of our parenting and on every quality of our children. The trouble is that we don't know, and cannot comprehend, the full scope of His parenthood. But we know many things about how He deals with His children, and thinking about and focusing on what we can emulate will bring about many positive things and prevent or overcome many negative ones. Said another way, following the parenting model and example of our Heavenly Father can help us give His children what He wants them to have and to steer clear of many potential parenting pitfalls even as it helps us dig ourselves out of pits we have already fallen into. Here is a short list of the positive possibilities and the negative cleansers just to get you thinking and connecting.

What Remembering God's Parenting Pattern Helps Us Bring to Pass

Better, more effective goal setting, for us and for our children. We can adopt God's goals for mortality and follow His method of spiritual creation. And, like He did, we can let our children set their own goals.

Better communication of children with you and with siblings. Shared responsibility breeds communication, and kids who share responsibility and help each other grow up as friends.

Good choices. Like God did, we can give our children choices that allow growth and the accepting of challenge.

Individual confidence and family security. Kids who are recognized as unique and who know where their boundaries are can discover their truest selves and feel grounded and secure.

Better obedience. To follow and obey is a choice and a joy, both in God's plan and in ours.

Covenant keeping. Making decisions and commitments in advance is the best way to avoid temptation.

Self-discipline and learning to work and handle money and other responsibilities. God gave us an environment that rewards effort and self-governance, and we can do the same.

What It Helps Our Children Avoid or Overcome

Entitlement. Having what we want, when we want it, and thinking everything is owed to us was never part of God's plan for us, nor should it be part of ours for our kids.

Laziness. Heavenly Father's approach leaves no room for idleness. Neither should ours.

Dishonesty. The reward for truth must always be greater than the punishment for the deed one has confessed.

Whining and complaining. Complaints happen more in situations of compulsion than when there is agency and choice.

Being spoiled by grandparents. Grandparents need to buy into your responsibility-giving approach so they don't become an easier way for kids to get what they want.

Guilt and secrecy. Children who commit to and are rewarded for truth, and who understand how to repent, will not carry around the guilt and secrets that undermine their happiness.

Bad choices. Knowing God's pattern for making good decisions can trump the peer pressure that is responsible for most bad decisions.

INTERMISSION
Why It's Worth All the Effort

We know it is a bit quirky, but we always like to put a short intermission halfway through our books. It gives us a chance to take a breath, think together as writers and readers about where we are going, and reflect a little on the first act as we anticipate the second.

Our particular reason for a little break in this book is to give you a pep talk. Don't be overwhelmed or let guilt or discouragement flag you at this point. No one should attempt every idea in this book. You shouldn't even try. It's not about checking everything off a list or becoming perfect at anything. No one can remember everything he should be or wants to do all the time.

Let us remind you: The main thing we are trying to do with this volume is change how we *think* about parenting and about our kids. It's the insights and the perspectives that count. Don't beat yourself up about not being able to do everything and try everything. Just pick ideas that appeal and apply what you can. But let your *understanding* and your *thoughts* about your kids change and upgrade. That doesn't take time, it just takes focus.

And at this point in the book, instead of running out of gas, getting discouraged, or feeling guilty—*do the opposite*. Reflect for a minute on the fact that your children are both your joy and your most important stewardship. Rejoice in the fact, and be thankful and calm about it.

By now, we hope you realize that this is not just a parenting book, but a book on priorities—on prioritizing our kids and also on prioritizing the spiritual. You have likely figured out that it is not only parenting solutions we've been talking about, it is perspectives for life that can make *us*, as well as our children, happier and more fulfilled. And you have probably already sensed that it is also a book on timing and on the seasons of life. The full-blooming "summer" of life is the fleeting time that we have our children in our homes with us. We will still have our jobs and our entertainments and our golf games in the autumn, but the kids will be gone. We must implement and prioritize these changes and ideas in the summer, because it is the only season when we can!

> *Parenting is the core stewardship of mortality and the thing most directly connected and relevant to our eternal salvation and returning to God.*

Parenting, we know through the restored gospel, is not just another skill to be worked on, like managing our finances or improving our gardening or even serving in our Church calling. Parenting is the core stewardship of mortality and the thing most directly connected and relevant to our eternal salvation and returning to God.

And what helps us parent better is understanding the clear differentiation between means and ends that the gospel gives us. Within the gospel, families and children are the end; jobs and houses and cars and money and all the other things of this world are just the means. We use them to help us with the goal and the purpose which centers on family.

Even the Church and its programs is a means that helps us toward the end result of eternal families. President Harold B. Lee uses an analogy of the Church and its organization as the *scaffolding* that helps in the building process.[1]

There is a wonderful congruency in *acting on* and *doing* what we believe.

People everywhere say (in public opinion polls) that family is the most important thing to them, yet it is just lip service if their lives and their priorities do not match what they say. In the Church we know more deeply and more specifically why families are the most important thing and why children are the most important stewardship, so it is even more crucial that we "walk the talk" and make how we live and how we parent match up with what we believe.

To do that, we must become, in a way, contrarians with the world— reversing the means and the ends, and seeing the job as a support for the family rather than the family as a slave or second fiddle to a career. We must find the courage of our convictions to sacrifice the approval, the applause, and the accolades of the world in favor of the approval of God as we prioritize the most important stewardship He has given for us.

But, as with so many sacrifices, what we get far outweighs what we give up.

Because it's not just about doing our duty and being righteous. It's about *joy* and *love*, the very things we were sent here to gain, the very purposes of mortality. It's about joy and love for us as well as for our children!

Think for a minute: Is there anything less joyous and less loving than "no children allowed"? Do you sense the stiff, staleness of people who are rarely exposed to the sparkle and spontaneity of kids?

As grandparents, the two of us now see it more clearly than ever— how much laughter and tears and love are missing when there are no kids around. And we know more surely than ever that family is the center of life.

Children are a source of joy! Not always pleasantness, and rarely easiness, but real, up-and-down, roller-coaster joy.

And joy, according to Nephi (2 Nephi 2:25), is the very reason for mortality, the very purpose of earth life. We have always felt that there were four levels of joy: First, the joy of just being in mortality, having the beauty of the earth and the freedom of agency. Second, the added joy of loving and of doing—of relationships and achievements. Third, the fuller joy of understanding the "why" and of knowing our purpose here and being guided by the eternal truths of the gospel, and fourth, the greatest joy of feeling God's love and His approval of what we are doing. The stewardship of children helps with and enhances each of the levels of joy.

These four types of joy correspond interestingly with four ascending "love" levels (which, once again, are totally affected by children): First, the love of the earth and of just being here on it. Second, the love that is deepened and made unconditional by our family commitments and stewardships. Third, the love that is made even more complete by understanding purpose and being a conscious part of God's plan, and fourth, feeling the pure love of Christ as we earn God's approval and the presence of His Spirit.

Motivated by these four levels of joy and of love . . . read on!

SOLUTION
3

Remember Your Direct Channel to the Father

Understand that we are mere mortal "babysitters" who can appeal directly to the real Parent. *Could there ever be a more effectual and answer-deserving prayer than this: "Father, help me to understand and to do what is best for this, thy child."*

When we write books together, we often divide up the chapters with one of us taking the lead on each. We fought (nicely) over this one because we both feel that this spiritual solution may be the one that has made the most difference in our own family. Linda finally let me lead out with a story, but the rest of the chapter is a joint effort.

This is, in some ways, a more personal story than we would normally tell, but it makes the main point of this third spiritual solution better than anything else we know.

A quick way to become well and truly scared is to see deep and puzzled fear in your doctor's eyes. That's what I was seeing after rushing Linda, six months pregnant, pale as a sheet, and hemorrhaging heavily, into the tiny district hospital in Epsom, Surrey, England. The only doctor there was a Pakistani intern who spoke hardly any English.

But he didn't need words because his eyes said it all. He had not seen anything like this before, and he did not know what to do. He pushed Linda's gurney into the small, outdated-looking emergency room to try to stop the bleeding, and I ran to the lobby and the pay phone to call Dr. Gordon in London. (This was long before cell phones, which becomes terrifyingly significant later in this story.)

Dr. Gordon had been introduced to me by our good friend, Dr. Rhodes Boyson, a member of Parliament, who had been sympathetic a few months earlier when I told him I was a bit worried about the obstetrics in the little country town where our mission home was. "Dr. Gordon," Rhodes had said, "is the preeminent OB-GYN doctor in this country." I had planned to call Dr. Gordon the following month, so I had his number in my wallet.

I got him on the line and told him what was happening. He said he would come immediately and that the trip to Epsom from London usually took forty-five minutes to an hour.

I paced and prayed and waited and hoped the intern wouldn't do anything to make things worse. Finally I burst into the emergency room and found that the bleeding had subsided somewhat.

Dr. Gordon, driving a fast Jaguar, made it in just over a half hour and soon had the hemorrhaging stopped and transfusions going. "Placenta previas are unpredictable," he said, "but every day we can keep the baby in there will improve the chances of survival." I walked out with him, and he jumped in his car and was off, heading back to London.

The relief I felt vanished as I walked back into the little hospital and heard the loud, anxious voices of two nurses and the intern. "She is bleeding again," one of the nurses said as she ran back *into* the emergency room and slammed the door behind her. "You can't come in, it's worse than before."

I stumbled outside and knelt down in a little grove of trees across the street, and prayed as I never had before—for my wife and partner, for the baby, for life in both cases.

As I prayed, I thought about earlier, connected prayers. One was the year before, when we prayed about whether we should have another child here in the mission field. We were (as all mission presidents are) over our heads in a lot of ways, but the answer had come clearly that another spirit was ready to join our family. And once we were pregnant, a constant prayer was for a choice and noble spirit, for a good pregnancy and a healthy baby, and for Linda's strength and well-being as she continued to mother our other four children and be the mission mother to 240 missionaries. And we had prayed often for good medical care, because it was not that easy to find in that place and at that time.

I was jarred out of my pleading prayer in the little grove by the sound of screeching tires. I looked up and saw Dr. Gordon's white Jaguar careening back into the little parking lot. I ran and jerked open his car door and blurted out what had happened. He took the front steps two at a time, ripping off his jacket and rolling up his shirt sleeves as he ran.

Less than ten minutes later, the emergency door opened and out came the same nurse. She looked right at me, smiled, and said, "That's why they call him 'Flash Gordon,' I guess. That was the fastest C-section I have ever seen. You have a really small little son, but he looks good, and so does your wife."

I found out later that virtually all the oxygenating blood had drained from the placenta and the baby was dying. Linda could have died too, but for an almost unbelievably fast emergency cesarean.

"Why did you come back?" I asked Dr. Gordon as I walked him to his car for the second time that day.

"I really don't know," he said. "I was halfway to London on the motorway and I had this overwhelmingly strong feeling."

The story really doesn't end there. Jonah was nine weeks early in a day when babies that premature usually did not survive. Later that same night, I put my hands through the sealed incubator into the built-in white gloves and gave Jonah a name so that the six elders from the office and I could give him a priesthood blessing of health and healing.

The little guy was in the hospital for forty days and forty nights, but he grew stronger every day and came home to the mission home a healthy baby.

Miracles? Without question! But what I remember most about all those connected prayers and blessings is the clarity of feeling. I knew I was talking directly to the Lord. There were no intermediaries, no links in the priesthood chain. I was the father and steward and patriarch of this family, and my prayers and His answers were direct and clear. This little son was really His son, and He cared about him even more than I did.

> *A surrogate parent, a mortal babysitter really, petitioning the true Father offers a singular and unique genre of prayer, a special kind of stewardship communication that is as direct and effectual as the prophet praying for the Church.*

I had felt that clarity and direct communication when we prayed about whether to have this baby. I felt it again when we prayed for a choice and noble spirit and again when I prayed for Linda's health and to find good medical care. And I felt it with all my heart as I pleaded from that little grove of trees to bring a doctor back, fast, in a white Jaguar.

But it's not just these kinds of life-and-death prayers that receive that pure, direct clarity from God. It is any sincere prayer where a parent is praying for a son or daughter.

A surrogate parent, a mortal babysitter really, petitioning the true Father offers a singular and unique *genre* of prayer, a special kind of stewardship communication that is as direct and effectual as the prophet praying for the Church.

Not all prayers are answered in the way we wish they could be, but prayer is the ultimate spiritual solution, and in this chapter we will explore various ways that prayer can be approached in a family setting and in the attitude of a child seeking help from a Father who has sent another of His children into the care of the first.

INSIGHTS

"More things are wrought by prayer than this world dreams of," said Alfred, Lord Tennyson.[1]

Prayer happens on so many levels and for so many reasons, but if we were to view it as a spectrum, with the least appropriate, least-chance-of-being-answered prayers on one end and the most appropriate, sure-to-be-answered prayers on the other end, a parent's prayer about a child (a prayer for insight, for help, for a child's need) would be on the extreme "most" end of the spectrum.

Indeed, the most frequently repeated admonition in all of scripture is to *ask!*

Having given us our agency, God cannot impose or capriciously, arbitrarily, or unilaterally dump answers or blessings on us without violating or interfering with that agency. As in the famous painting of Christ, who stands at door with no door handle and knocks, so it is with God. We must open the door and let Him in.

Because He is our Heavenly Father, He wants to give us all that He has, but because He is God, He will never give unwisely or in a way that undermines our agency. But when we ask, the initiative is ours, and He can pour out blessings on us according to His perfect knowledge of our needs.

The "Auto-Correction" of Prayer

I was talking to another mom who told me of a very difficult problem she was having with her daughter. She was a faithful Church member, so at one point I asked her if she had prayed about the problem.

"Not yet," she said, "I feel I have to do all I can about it myself before I burden the Lord with it."

An interesting response. On the one hand I admired her for her initiative and for wanting to be proactive about it. On the other hand, this was a very difficult problem, and she clearly needed divine help.

Do we sometimes get too caught up with admonitions such as, "Pray as though everything depended on God. Work as though everything depended on you"?[2] Or do we struggle with scriptures like "study it out in your mind" (D&C 9:8), or, as in this mother's case, a reluctance to "burden" the Lord?

Of course, we should not ask frivolously, and, of course, our own thoughts and efforts can help and will likely make our prayers more specific and more earnest.

But the Lord asks us to cast our burdens on Him, and He wants to help and lead us and even to intervene when the worry is beyond our ability to solve or resolve.

The wonderful thing about prayer, and it seems particularly true with the prayer of a parent for a child, is that it is "self-correcting." As we pray, we sometimes are given to know more about what it is we are praying for and to better understand what we should be asking Heavenly Father for.

One mother prayed about her son's poor grades in school and, as she listened for answers, she felt impressed to have his hearing checked. She soon discovered that his learning difficulty had everything to do with his ears and nothing to do with his brain.

A dad praying that his son would do better on his little league team

92

began to realize, during the prayer, that the boy wanted to do art after school rather than baseball.

A mom praying for her teenager's testimony felt inspired that his faith was fine and that it was a new friend that was the problem.

Heavenly Father essentially is telling us to come unto Him in prayer (particularly for our children), and the Spirit will teach us for what we should ask.

Let's face it, we sometimes don't know enough to know what to ask for. Pray anyway, and the Spirit will inspire us first on the questions and then on the answers.

> *Prayer is "self-correcting." As we pray, we sometimes are given to know more about what it is we are praying for and to better understand what we should be asking Heavenly Father for.*

It is never "too soon to pray." If we are asking for the wrong thing or if there is preparation or action we should take along with our prayer, we will feel and learn of those things even as we pray.

Better to be too early to pray than too late!

Listening and Note-Taking in Prayer

On my first mission, I had the privilege of being a guide at the Church's pavilion at the New York World's Fair. My companion and I lived in a large high-rise apartment complex in Queens where all the World's Fair missionaries were supervised by a General Authority, Elder Bernard P. Brockbank, as well as by our mission president. Elder Brockbank, with his wife Frances, lived in the same big apartment building where we did.

I came to admire Elder Brockbank. He was quite a guy. As we missionaries would guide the throngs of people through the Mormon Pavilion, there occasionally would be one or two who wanted to dispute the Church's claims, and Elder Brockbank instructed us not to argue or even to try to answer them. "Just bring them back to my office," he said.

One of my favorite experiences was escorting feisty, angry people into his office and watching them walk out a few minutes later, calmer, smiling, humbled, and with a look on their face that was somewhere between puzzlement and respect.

One night, back at the building where we lived, as my companion and I were getting ready for bed, a knock came at our door. I opened it, and there was Elder Brockbank standing in the hall in his nightshirt. "Frances is in Salt Lake this week," he said. "May I join you elders for evening prayer?"

We invited him in, knelt down, and he asked me to pray. I rambled on with what I thought was a suitably thorough prayer in his presence, trying not to leave anything out. At some point in the prayer, I heard the unmistakable sound of a pencil writing rapidly on paper. Not daring to peek, I continued on, horror-struck that my greenie companion had gotten impatient, didn't really understand who this was that we were kneeling with, and had started his nightly epistle to his girlfriend. But when I finally wrapped up the prayer and opened my eyes, it was Elder Brockbank who had filled up most of the top page of a yellow pad with bold, scribbled writing.

At that point, my nineteen-year-old brain formed another theory: He had evaluated my prayer! I imagined maybe I got a B on content, perhaps a C on sincerity.

Elder Brockbank said nothing, other than to thank us for letting him join us, and he moved toward the door to leave. I was much too intimidated to ask him about what he had been writing.

He actually went out into the hall, almost closed the door, and then opened it again, looked right at me with his trademark twinkle in his eye, and uttered a couple of sentences I will never forget. "Elder, you look a little curious about my yellow pad. It's simple really. You see, I'm getting a little older now and my memory's not perfect. I find that if I don't take notes on what the Lord tells me, I'm likely to forget some things."

I lay awake a long time that night, staring at the ceiling with my eyes wide open and wondering at the awesome simplicity of what I had just learned. This man talks to God. God talks back to him. He listens. He takes notes. Prayer is a dialogue! Prayer is real!

If you or we had an audience with the prophet, we would do more listening than talking. We do have an audience with God whenever we pray, and our subject matter is anything but trivial; it is about our children, it is about His children. Listen, hear, remember, and follow!

Think about getting yourself a special notebook or perhaps even a bound "blank book" for prayer notes so that you can go back and review frequently what the Lord has answered and what promptings He has given.

> *Get yourself a special notebook or perhaps even a bound "blank book" for prayer notes so that you can go back and review frequently what the Lord has answered and what promptings He has given.*

One of the most faith-promoting things I have in my personal life as a father and a priesthood holder is a small book that I started using years ago to keep track of the things I was praying for. A large percentage of my requests were for my children, or about my children. As I look back now, over these many decades since I started making those notes, there is not one single prayer that has not been answered. The blessings did not always come in the ways I had anticipated, and the answers were not always the ones I wanted, but *all* of the prayers have been answered.

And I am so glad I have that little book as a testament of what I have asked for and what I have been given.

Fear God, and Not Your Kids

It is amazing how many parents seem to be afraid of their kids. A friend of ours glanced at her daughter's open diary one day. ("I wasn't really snooping," she said. "It was just laying there and I couldn't help it.") What she read took her breath away because it was about experimentation with drugs and with sex. She couldn't tell if some of it was about things that had already happened or things that were being thought about.

"What do I do?" she asked us. "I'm trying so hard to be her friend, and I'm so afraid that if she knows I looked in her journal she won't trust me anymore."

The answer is, first of all, your daughter doesn't need you to be her friend, she needs you to be her parent. And you should be far more worried that she has not trusted you now and in the past enough to tell you what is going on than you are about whether she will trust you in the future because you looked at her journal. Count yourself lucky that you got some clues and find out what is going on!

Another dad bought a car he couldn't afford because his son didn't think the one he had was "cool." And another family got their eight- and ten-year-olds iPhones and iPads and the latest Wii game because the kids told them they were the only ones in their classes without these necessities.

Parents, we are stewards of God, not servants of our kids. Our duty and our task is not to please our kids but to please God. Our goal is to raise responsible and righteous kids who respect us, not self-indulged, entitled kids who think we are cool.

Don't ever think (or let your kids think) that there are some things that they are doing or thinking that you do not need to know. "Privacy" is not a constitutional right of kids from their parents!

Explain to your children that you are their steward. Stewardship is, at its core, a simple principle that even young children can understand,

and by the time a child is baptized, he or she is ready for a serious discussion with parents about the things he is a steward over. In with that discussion, talk about the fact that the most important stewardship that Heavenly Father gives us on this earth is the stewardship over children—which is really a stewardship over the temporal upbringing of a few of our spiritual brothers and sisters. Once children understand this, it will be easier for them to understand why you need to know everything, why nothing is off-limits, and why all they have in the "need to know" file of their brain should be open to you because, as their steward, you need to know it all!

The most important tool that any spiritual steward has is prayer, and the application of prayer to our specific stewardships may be the most powerful spiritual skill we can ever learn. LDS parents need to strive to become proficient, even masterful, at all of the kinds of prayer available to us—private prayer, husband and wife prayer, family prayer, and one-on-one prayer with our children.

The Combining of Works and Grace

One of the most amazing benefits of direct stewardship prayer for and about our children is that it manages to combine works and grace.

We often pray for something regarding our families or our kids, and what we get in answer is a prompting of something we should *do* (works). Yet at other times, maybe on occasion of our deepest and most humble and desperate prayers, instead of a prompting to do something, we sometimes—when it is the Lord's will—get a miracle or a direct intervention of some kind (grace).

The point to remember is that God, the real and Heavenly Father, wants us, the surrogate, substitute parents, to do all we can, and then to rely on Him for the needs we cannot meet. One good definition of parental faith is that we get as close to what we want on our own power, and trust Him to fill the gap that is still left between where we are and where we want to be . . . or the gap between what we can do for our children and what the full extent of their needs are.

Only the Spirit can fill these gaps, and it is our earnest stewardship prayers that trigger and call for the Spirit.

APPLICATIONS

Couple Prayers and Variations

To those fortunate enough to be two-parent families, spouse or "couple prayers" are both a remarkable privilege and an indispensable tool of guidance.

Early in our marriage, as we knelt together by our bed for our prayer each night, one of us would be the voice, and the other would sometimes worry about the things the pray-er left out.

One night we got into a discussion about trying to make our couple prayers more like an actual meeting with Heavenly Father—the two of us, stewards over each other and over our children, and partners in the goal of creating an eternal family, coming together with the Managing Partner to discuss the issues and needs of the day and to present our feelings and gratitude. The idea of a nightly three-way partnership meeting made things seem more real to us, and the concept of it caused us to modify the structure of our prayer in an interesting way.

One of us would begin the verbal prayer, and when finished with the thanks-giving and the asking parts would, instead of closing the prayer, simply squeeze the other's hand. The other would then continue with his or her own thoughts, thanks, and requests. Then another hand squeeze to go back to any other thoughts of the first, and so forth until both were finished and then the one who did not open the prayer would close it in the name of Jesus Christ. We also began to have more "listening pauses" where neither of us was talking and both were listening to any impressions or responses from the Managing Partner.

Whether you do it in precisely this way or not, it is useful (and wonderful) to perceive yourselves—as parents and as marriage partners—as part of a magnificent partnership with God, the giver of all stewardships and the Father of us all, in the goal of raising children.

We were trying to advise a young couple once, and their question was, "How can we continue to grow closer and closer to each other?" They felt that their two children were taking so much of their time and mental energy that they had no time for each other, and they wondered if there were some tricks or techniques for drawing closer to one another.

Instead of a technique or a trick, we gave them a concept. If a couple's partnership with God can be diagrammed with a triangle, with Heavenly Father at the top and the husband and wife at the two lower corners, then one way to draw closer as a couple is to each strive to move closer to God. As each moves up their side of the triangle that connects to God, you begin to find yourself, on the triangle and in reality, also becoming closer and closer to each other.

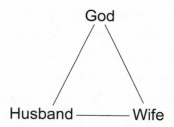

Family Prayers and Variations

If a couple's prayer is a private partnership meeting with the Managing Partner, then a family prayer is a group meeting with the true Father of us all!

The thing that sometimes disinterests kids in family prayers is that they are often long (when a parent gives them), somewhat formal, and frequently filled with a lot of words children may not understand. Plus it involves two things that most kids have a hard time with: Staying still and quiet and keeping their attention focused.

While nothing can substitute for a good, kneeling family prayer whenever possible before bedtime, there are some variations on the family prayer theme that can make prayer more enjoyable and more relevant and real for children.

Many LDS families try to have some kind of brief devotional before work, school, or any other events of the day. Getting up just a little earlier to allow a somewhat organized breakfast and "devo" is worth the effort, and generally concludes with a prayer aimed specifically at the events taking place that day.

The problem, of course, for so many families, is that different people leave at different times in the morning and throughout the day, and even getting everyone together for a moment is quite a challenge. In the days when our house was a busy madhouse of school, activities, lessons, games, and ins-and-outs at all hours, we got into the good habit of a "huddle prayer." As someone was leaving the house he would yell, "Huddle!" and anyone within earshot would hustle in and huddle like a football team for a brief prayer. Arms around each other, someone would offer a quick prayer for the safety and guidance of the person heading out and express love and gratitude. It would take just a few seconds and it put everyone in a more spiritual and loving frame of mind.

One morning we came to the stark realization that those huddles—wherein, among other things, we prayed for protection for our kids every day—really worked. One morning after we had sent two high school kids to school after a huddle, we got a frantic call from our thirteen-year-old Talmadge saying that fifteen-year-old Jonah had just been hit by a car while running across the street to the school.

As the long hours passed on that fateful day we realized that our prayers for protection truly were answered on Jonah's behalf. He was wearing a backpack with over thirty pounds of books which propelled him cleanly through the windshield of the car that hit him, and he flew into the lap of an unsuspecting little Hawaiian lady in the passenger seat. He missed the car frame by three inches.

One leg was shattered and all the ligaments in his other knee were destroyed, and there was really no reason that he should have lived through that accident except for the angels who were surely watching over him. Today Jonah's legs aren't pretty, but he is an extraordinary person and the father of four children, fulfilling his fabulous foreordination. We know that prayers like that are not always answered in the way we wish they were. In many accident cases, children are crippled, paralyzed, end up in a vegetative state, or even die, and prayers then begin to meet other kinds of needs. But we know that particular morning our prayer for protection in that huddle was answered!

Another family prayer variation is something some families call "synchronized prayer." At breakfast or in the brief morning devotional, a parent might state who has a big test, game, performance, or some other important event during the day. After finding out what time it begins, each family member, wherever he is, tries to remember to say a brief prayer for the family member at the start of the event.

Once in a while, when there is a particularly strong or urgent need, a family prayer that somewhat resembles a group meeting with Heavenly Father can be an impressionable and powerful experience. A family might kneel in a circle and hold hands and proceed in a manner similar to the "couple's prayer" mentioned earlier where one person finishes his thanks or requests and then squeezes the hand of the next person in the circle who continues the prayer.

Obviously, this should not become some kind of ritual or alternative prayer, and should not take over for the usual, traditional family prayer, but as a prayer for special times or needs, it can be useful. It can also teach children that all family prayers are times when all of the family prays, both those that are praying silently and the person who is speaking. Some families reserve this kind of prayer for Fast Sunday or other special occasions.

Family prayer with two or more small children can sometimes be enhanced by having all of the kids repeat the phrases of the prayer after the parent so that not just one of them is involved.

Some families have a "prayer record" where they keep track of the things they are remembering to be thankful for and the things they are asking for. They might keep a list of friends, neighbors, or ward members who are facing particular difficulties. They may, in a family home evening, even do some "prayer planning" where they discuss what things they want to remember to say thanks for and what things they want to ask for. This kind of discussion, of course, can cause children to be more thoughtful in prayers and to really think about what they are saying rather than just remembering and repeating frequent prayer phrases.

Fasting (Rejoicing) and Prayer

We have come, during our travels and speaking opportunities in the Middle East and Indonesia, to understand a bit better the more than a billion Muslims in the world and to realize how much we have in common with devout Muslim families. This is an easy conclusion to reach when you hear such things as, "I wish we were not so identified with our extremist elements," or "We take a lot of ridicule because we don't drink alcohol or use tobacco," or "We are so much stricter with our children than our less religious neighbors." About the tenth time you lose your bearings and think you are in Bountiful or Provo instead of Saudi or Bahrain, you realize how similar our cultures are, as well as our convictions.

When it comes to fasting, some Muslims really put us to shame. Ramadan, the annual spiritual festival, begins with thirty days of fasting (they eat nothing during the day—while the sun is up—for an entire month.) If you ask a devout family what the purpose of the fasting is, even the children know the answer: To make us feel humble . . . to make us remember God . . . to remind us that God gives us all we have . . . to help us forsake our sins and become better people.

Fasting, like the Word of Wisdom and like many other practical teachings of the Church, is becoming more popular and "in vogue" in the world around us as its benefits become more and more apparent and understood. Many people laud the physical benefits of giving the digestive system a rest, of purging and cleaning the body, and of slowing down and focusing the mind in the absence of food.

In the Church, the practice of a monthly fast, combined with the bearing of testimony and paying a fast offering to aid the poor, is a wonderful spiritual example of a "win-win situation." The welfare system and the poor among us benefit, and we benefit both physically and spiritually. And those who learn to fast with joy and purpose reap blessings both obvious and subtle.

How young can kids start fasting? It may vary with the child, but usually by the time of baptism and the age of accountability, kids are old enough not only to miss a meal without adverse effect, but to understand why they are doing it and what it can do for them.

To make fasting (or a "half-fast" which is what we often call missing one meal instead of two) the most relevant it can be to children, decide in advance, perhaps in the family home evening the Monday before, what you will be fasting for as a family.

Praying for Peace and Realizing That Calmness Is Contagious

One great key that many parents have learned is that the calmness and peace and awareness of the Spirit is contagious, particularly within a family setting. The problem is that the opposite is also true. When parents are stressed, uptight, nervous, or high-strung, children feel it and begin to feel and behave similarly. And, almost magically, when parents feel calm, at ease, filled with love, the children become more peaceful, more manageable, and more loving.

Many parents we know have specific methods for calming themselves, and many do it for the specific purpose of having that peace rub off on their kids. One dad, as he returned from work each day, would pull his car into the dark, quiet garage and just sit there for a few seconds, breathing deeply, relaxing, making a conscious effort to leave the concerns of work behind and focus on his love for his wife and children. Then he would say a brief, silent prayer and get up and walk into the house, preconditioned to look for the love and the good, and to overlook any chaos, tension, or negative energy that he might encounter.

A mom, surrounded by little kids, had a unique technique. She would periodically just lock herself in the bathroom for a few moments, do her own short version of a little meditation and prayer, and emerge a little calmer to take on the next challenge.

Still another mom, whenever she felt herself approaching her boiling point, would suddenly shut her eyes, bow her head, take a deep breath, murmur the universal calming mantra of "ohmmmmm" (which momentarily confused and quieted her kids), and say a brief, silent, on-the-spot prayer for peace. Then she would raise her head, open her eyes, smile widely at her children, and carry on.

"We Shape Our Buildings; Thereafter They Shape Us"

It was Winston Churchill who said the above quote,[3] and it is true even beyond what he may have meant by it.

If we are able to create a peaceful, calm, and orderly atmosphere in our homes, our children will become more manageable, more spiritual, and better behaved.

The trouble is that *kids* reside in homes, and kids are prone toward things that move the mood in opposite directions—things like fighting and yelling and letting their energy out in countless ways that are anything but calm.

You have probably heard some great (and slightly off-beat) ways that parents of young, feisty, energetic children have tried to instill a calmer, more peaceful spirit in their homes. Some try to keep soft classical music going "to tame the savage beast." Others try to "use our inside voices" or to have "silence contests" to see who can go the longest without saying anything at all.

We have tried a few desperate methods of our own. For a while we tried to have everyone whisper until breakfast started in order to begin the day in a calmer way. We would sit for a "quiet moment" holding hands around the dinner table before the blessing. We tried turning our palms up, closing our eyes and following our friend's idea of breathing the universal mantra of "ohmmmmm" as a signal for kids to join us for an "ohmmmmm" and to calm down. And one time, noticing that Christmas seemed to bring a kind of calm with it, we decided to leave a little Christmas

> *The best method is simply to pray more, and to pray harder, for the Spirit of Peace, for the Spirit of God, which is the Holy Ghost.*

tree up, right in the center of our round dining table, into the new year.

The problem, of course, with all these ideas is that they are artificial and rely on our ability to calm ourselves rather than relying on the calming spirit of the Holy Ghost. The best method is simply to pray more, and to pray harder, for the Spirit of Peace, for the Spirit of God, which is the Holy Ghost.

Special-Needs Kids

As much as all parents need prayer and the aid of the real Parent, the need is never so pronounced or so heartfelt as with a special-needs child.

We came face to face with this kind of special need when the expensive tests came back on our granddaughter, Lucy, confirming that she has a rare genetic syndrome called Bardet Biedl. In a nutshell, that means that unless research can get ahead of the diagnosis, this adorable, chubby, little blue-eyed princess will be blind sometime between the ages of nine and fifteen. Her intake of food will be an issue 24/7 as her body turns virtually everything she eats into fat. Perhaps there will be kidney and/or heart issues. When we heard the diagnosis, a dark cloud hung over us . . . not only Lucy's parents and four siblings but the entire extended family as we digested the news.

It's been two years since the diagnosis, and we have learned many things. Some are hard things, as we observe older children afflicted with Bardet Biedl struggle with obesity and grope their way along with white canes. Other things are hopeful, as we watch the progress of research that may save Lucy's sight and improve her life. We have gained admiration and respect for the children and parents we have met who are so courageously dealing with this challenge.

On our journey with our beloved Lucy and this syndrome we have also become aware of the enormous number of parents who are dealing with children with other special needs that are equally as difficult and in some cases vastly more so.

Childhood diabetes is now at epidemic levels, as is autism, ADHD, and eating disorders.

Our little five-year-old niece was just diagnosed with leukemia. As we write, her body has been flooded with the poison of chemotherapy and, after the administration of her steroids, her face and tummy look as though they have been blown up with a bicycle pump. Her hair is falling out. Her personality has changed, but she is still smiling and is teaching all of us with her courage.

The more we have immersed ourselves into the world of children with special needs, the more we have learned about the positive things these special needs do for families. If handled with spiritual insights, these challenges can lead to life's greatest blessings. This is all easy to say when you're not living with it day after day and year after year, but we think most parents and families who are would agree.

Keeping eternal perspectives in place is crucial and even mandatory in order to survive as we realize that some day we will see the purpose for the suffering as well as the joy that the pure love of Christ brings. Great love and added perspectives are gained as family members rally around with help and support and develop new levels of empathy. We also develop faith that the afflicted child is able to better fulfill his fore-ordinations through his trials. Again and again we see parents and families become refined through the fire that special-needs children bring.

And for those with special needs so profound that there is little hope in this world, what a joy it will be when family and friends meet on the other side of the veil and all can rejoice together with the glorious spiritual being who was trapped in a malfunctioning physical body!

"Can't Do" Prayers

Often, our speaking schedule brings us together or puts us on the same program with "motivational speakers." We enjoy their presentations, and we certainly see nothing wrong with positive mental attitudes and "can-do" mentalities.

But there is also a time for recognizing what we *can't* do and for the humility of acknowledging our profound need for God's help.

Abraham Lincoln said, "I have been driven many times upon my knees by the overwhelming conviction that I had nowhere else to go."[4]

We love the power and inspiration that often comes with the humility of a "can't-do" prayer where parents essentially say, "It's too much for me; it's more than I can handle; I am in over my head. Please, Father, help me."

Making Personal Prayer Real for Young Children

The prayers of small children frequently fall into two categories. They can be wonderful models of candor and sincerity and faith. Or they can be a string of repetitive phrases learned from hearing adults pray.

There are two very simple ways to make prayer more real and more relevant to a very small child.

First, have a little talk with a child before his prayer. Discuss what He is thankful for and why God might have given him certain things, and talk about what blessings he thinks he needs and how God might be able to help.

Second, ask the child what he or she thinks God feels when we pray. What does He feel when we say thanks? What does He feel when we ask forgiveness? What does He feel when we ask for blessings? Help the child to think of God as a real father, listening to His children as they pray.

Let Your Children Hear You Pray for Them

Not long after I came home from my first mission in New York City, the Church held a special meeting for returned missionaries in the upper room/assembly hall of the Logan Temple. Two or three of the brethren spoke to us, and then it was Elder Harold B. Lee's turn.

He was dressed in his temple clothes, and instead of speaking to us, he came to the pulpit, bowed his head, and said a wonderful prayer for all of us there assembled. It was a specific prayer, asking for many particular things that returning missionaries need and focusing on many of the concerns and adjustments we were experiencing.

I will never forget how it felt to hear that Apostle pray for me. It must have been a bit like what the Nephites felt when the Savior Himself prayed for them.

Our children need to hear us pray for them in this same, specific, personal manner. Don't always call on a child to offer family prayer. Often, you should be the voice, and give thanks for particular and unique things about each child, and then ask for help on the individual needs or worries of each child.

Keep it as short as your children's attention span, but make it strong and earnest, and use your faith as you pray. It will impact your children twice—once by helping them feel your love and personal concern for them, and then by drawing down heaven's blessings on them via your sincere requests.

IMPACTS

What It Helps Us Bring to Pass

Prayer, we must come to understand, is not just about saying thank you and asking for things we think we need. It is a principle of enormous power. It is the essence of bringing things to pass, often things far beyond the reach of our own feeble powers. There is no limit to the things prayer can be applied to, but for our parenting purposes here, let's consider some of the things that our direct, personal appeals from parent to Parent can bring to pass.

Better personal prayers and the armor of God for our children. Practice makes perfect, and prayer will protect and guide them all of their lives.

Family loyalty and bonding. Family prayer binds and bonds members together and helps children to feel an identity larger than themselves.

A stronger testimony. Both our own convictions and those of our children grow stronger as prayer becomes an ever more real part of our lives.

Teamwork and unity between parents. Prayer together and the common cause of children draw husband and wife together.

Calmness and peace. Everyone seeks it, but only the Spirit can bring it.

Confident humility within our children. These are often thought of as opposites, yet our relationship to God brings both.

Direct personal revelation. God will guide us as directly in our stewardship of children as He does the prophet in his stewardship of the Church.

What It Helps Us Avoid or Overcome

It is impossible, of course, to anticipate every negative thing that could happen to your children and your family and to pray that they won't happen. But we can indeed think about the dangers our kids face, and our prayers and our children's prayers can literally protect them spiritually and allow them (and us) to skirt some of the pending errors in their path or to help them pull away from the grip of a sin that might already have grabbed hold of them. Among the many trials and temptations of this life, prayer will be of help in the following areas.

Being swayed and influenced by friends. Our prayers and our children's prayers can inoculate against peer pressure.

Inactivity and apathy. The Spirit is what keeps them at bay.

Rebellion. Instead of a battle of wills, stewardship prayer can make it a battle of Spirit where the right wins.

Parental loneliness. Raising kids alone can feel terribly isolated, but raising them with God can give strength and often prompts us to discuss and work in tandem with other parents.

Fear of our kids. Instead of trying to win them over and please them, we can work at pleasing God and winning our children's respect.

The pressure and self-reliance of "going it alone." Just admitting that the challenge of raising a child is too great for us begins the humble process of seeking and receiving God's help.

Cookie-cutter, one-size-fits-all parenting ideas. Going to God for insights on our own children helps us avoid oversimplified or pat answers.

SOLUTION

4

Remember the Church's "Scaffolding"

❧

Take full advantage of all the help, support, and guidance the Church can give. *As we look back on any success we may have had in raising our children, one humbling thought is always crystal clear: We could not have done it without the Church!*

We mentioned earlier President Lee's analogy of the Church organization as "scaffolding." Does that diminish or understate what the Church is?

We think not! Tall, straight, beautiful buildings cannot be built without scaffolding. The scaffolding eventually comes down, but not until the structure is complete. The Church is God's organization here on earth, during the construction period of our families, and it will not be needed in the hereafter only because it has done its job here in this world and families have progressed enough to return to God's presence.

The question for now is: Are we making full use of this wonderful, divine scaffolding?

The ancient Igbo culture of Nigeria has a proverb, "Ora na azu nwa," which means it takes a village to raise a child. The Igbos also name their children "Nwa ora" which means child of the community.[1]

A negative twist on the same idea pretty well describes one of the biggest worries of parents today: "Children are a product of their cultures and their communities." Our children grow up in a peer-pressure culture, in a media and video game culture, in a culture of entitlement and bail outs and something for nothing. Their communities are online. Their influencers are advertisers, Facebook friends, and Hollywood and various purveyors of violence and pornography.

But let's shift back to the positive. Change one word, and the Nigerian proverb works perfectly for the LDS culture today: "It takes a ward to raise a child."

Can you imagine trying to raise a child in today's world without the ward or branch? Without the bishop and the Young Men and Young Women programs and the home teachers and the visiting teachers and the scout leader and the coaches and the advisors and the Sunday school teachers? Can you imagine trying to raise a child without the Aaronic priesthood quorums and the Duty to God awards and the Young Women Personal Progress program and the treks and the youth conferences and the camps and the outings and the commemorations? Can you imagine trying to raise a child without the ward family? Or without your children's friends in the ward or your friends in the ward who know your kids and care about them and say and do little encouraging things that you don't even know about?

It takes a ward to raise a family!

We know of some people who got a work transfer that put them in a location that was more than an hour from the nearest ward. "Well," they thought, "such is life. We will get to church at least once a month and hold our own the rest of the time. We know the gospel, and we can teach it to our children."

Some things they missed right away. Other things they kidded themselves into thinking they were doing fine without. Over time, it took its predictable toll. The kids developed the wrong kind of friends (not to suggest that all our kids' friends should be from the ward, or even from the Church, but what a centering, faith-holding force those "old reliables" can be), and had no backup role models and no consistent progress in gospel knowledge and study. Most of all, the parents started feeling more and more isolated and alone. They developed friends, but not "soul-friends" with whom they could share anything and everything, and they felt absolutely lonely and vulnerable when it came to the constant battle of trying to influence their children more than they were influenced by other sources. *Oh how they missed the ward!*

Like all good things, it is easy to take the ward for granted and criticize its imperfections. Not everyone is a good influence. No wards are perfect and some pose difficult situations for kids. Not all Church kids (or leaders) are good influences. We often wish for different teachers or youth leaders than what we have. Some programs we might feel are wasting our kids' time and ours. Our children sometimes can't find friends their age with similar interests or don't even have friends their age in the ward. In addition, wards and branches in the "mission field" may be filled with kids whose families are not members and who may be struggling with social and emotional issues that will require more of our kids than they get in return.

Still, it is hard to measure all the ways that the Church backs us up and helps us raise our children!

If we have never lived without it, we may tend to take all the ward does for us for granted. After all, we're entitled to it aren't we, as members of the Church?

Instead of taking it for granted, we need to fully appreciate and *use* it.

What we need to do is to remember that our children are our stewardship, our responsibility, that the buck stops here, and that we can't count on the ward or the Church to do our job for us. But, having said (and remembered) that, we should avail ourselves to all of the support and backup that the Church offers us.

Don't take the "general contractor" approach to parenting where we say, "Hey, the plumber and electrician and carpenter and other subcontractors (bishop, priesthood leader, scoutmaster, teacher) will do all the actual work, I just have to be sure my kids are there."

Instead, take the "scaffolding" approach. Fully use, appreciate, and coordinate with all that the Church does (and can do) to support your family.

> *Take the "scaffolding" approach. Fully use, appreciate, and coordinate with all that the Church does (and can do) to support your family.*

INSIGHTS

The "Second Ring"

As a young man, I once wrote a piece called "The Second Ring" as an attempt to describe and illustrate how enormously important the Church and the ward is in terms of supporting our parenting and helping us to raise responsible and righteous children. Here is an excerpt of what I wrote.

Some things are too big and some are too small.

Our families are the most important things we belong to, but they are often too small to give us all the associations we need or the temporal or spiritual help we may need to protect us from the negative influences around us or help us with the difficulties we face.

We also belong to a society—and are citizens of our city, state, and country. But these are too large and too impersonal to nurture us spiritually, to reach out to us personally, to become part of our identity, or to enhance our scope of self.

We need a second ring, a middle level, a close, neighborhood group to which we can belong, from which we can draw help, comfort, understanding, concern, and stimulation, and to which and through which we can give of ourselves.

To some extent, a workplace or a school can be this second ring, but the emphasis of the workplace is economic, and the focus of the school is academic. We need a second ring where the emphasis is personal and spiritual.

We need the second ring of the Church.

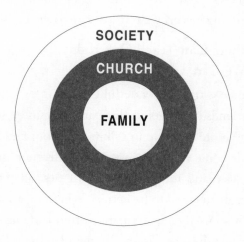

"Strangers" That Help Us Raise Our Children

We were late for a flight one day with all of our children (actually, of course, they were *why* we were late), and we had failed to get preassigned seats. There were just enough seats left on the full flight, but no two were together. We wailed to the boarding agent about needing to sit together, but it was too late to do anything. The kids were spread all over the airplane.

It was the best flight we had ever had!

Each child was sandwiched in between two strangers, and none of those usually boisterous and embarrassing little kids dared to make a peep. The two of us read our magazines and enjoyed the anonymity and the solitude.

We liked it so well that after that we often intentionally spread the kids out on planes. (We told them, to their horror, that it was so that they could do missionary work with the person they sat by.)

And when it comes to the Church or the ward, not only do strangers (or people our kids don't know as well as they know us—like which buttons to push) keep children quiet and orderly, they have a "social distance" that allows them to say things to our children better (and with our children listening better) than if we were to say those same things.

Sometimes Others Can Teach Our Kids Better Than We Can

Social distance is truly a wonderful thing.

Often our friends or others in the ward have more social distance, and therefore are more effective in talking with our children about certain things. Kids come home from youth conference, scout and girls' camp, or Young Men and Young Women activities full of the light of the gospel and are truly inspired to be better, do better, and think better!

Our kids get so used to us that they often tune us out, whereas a priesthood quorum advisor or Young Women leader or Primary teacher gets their attention long enough to get some of the same things we say to really get through to our children.

The way to take full advantage of this is not only to appreciate it, but to milk it! Be aware of who your kids' teachers and advisors are. Debrief your children about what they are learning. Visit with the teachers and advisors to learn what their impressions are of your kids and what they might have learned about them. Coordinate your own efforts with what teachers and ward leaders are doing. Work with the goals being set in the Young Men Duty to God or the Young Women Personal Progress programs. Team up and enjoy mutual support with youth leaders as you work together on your children!

Think of the ward as your backup, your support, and your child-rearing team!

Using, but Not Abusing, the "General Contractor" Approach

We warned earlier of the "general contractor" approach to parenting where we supervise what gets done but don't actually do very much of it ourselves.

When we are out in the world speaking, we use this as a pejorative term—as something to avoid. We stress that, in parenting, "the buck stops here," meaning the responsibility buck for the children stopping with the parents, with us, and that a general contractor approach is doomed to fail.

But there is a positive twist to that model in the context of the Church. What if we could all be the kind of "hands-on" general contractor who takes full personal responsibility and knows he has to do much of the work (particularly the essential tasks) himself? What could be better than having all kinds of subcontractors, from youth advisors to teachers to the "construction superintendent" bishop?

Help with Standards

We used to love what was called "Standards Nights" when our children were in Young Men and Young Women and a dynamic speaker would present teenagers with compelling reasons for staying morally clean and pure before marriage.

Although that still happens occasionally today, that message has largely been transferred to frequent references to the *For the Strength of Youth* booklet and lessons from leaders full of good ideas and constant reminders of the importance of remaining chaste before marriage.

Of course, this kind of help from the ward and the youth leaders does not release us from sitting down to have the "Big Talk" about sex with our children when they are young. Studies show that the most important factor in the lives of kids who avoid early, dangerous sexual experimentation is intimate talks with parents. The more parents communicate about sex to children, the less likely they are to experiment and try things they shouldn't.

Take the responsibility for talking to your kids about morality and standards in all their forms. And then be grateful for the ward leaders and youth leaders who back you up!

Priesthood Leaders as Surrogate Parents

When a boy loses his father at age fifteen as I did, he looks for any chance to honor and remember that father, and I now have the opportunity to do exactly that, with the permission of Elder Quentin Cook of the Quorum of the Twelve Apostles.

When Elder Cook was a boy, a bit older than I, but growing up as I did in Logan, Utah, he had a father who was a wonderful man but completely inactive in the Church. My dad was in the bishopric in our ward where young Quentin attended, and Dad often asked the young deacon if he could take him on father-and-son's outings. Always complimentary of Brother Vern Cook, Quentin's father, who was a kind and wonderful man but who just didn't come to church, my dad often filled in for him with Quentin and was a part of keeping the young boy active and interested in the Church and the gospel.

In Elder Cook's words: "I have a great appreciation for Richard's father, Dean Eyre. He made a significant contribution to me at an important stage of my life. He was very wise in being supportive of my Church activity, but at the same time he recognized the outstanding qualities of my father. He was a source of encouragement throughout my teenage years. He was a great example in every way and we became very good friends."

APPLICATIONS

It's one thing to appreciate the ward family and the support of the Church and the guidance of its prophets. It is another, greater thing to actually and consciously *use* these assets and advantages to help raise our children . . . and to coordinate and synergize with them in maximizing what they do and what we do for our kids.

Debriefing after Classes, Camps, and Activities

Are you looking for an enjoyable and possibly humorous Sunday dinner-time entertainment that may lead to a lovely in-depth discussion about what was learned that day in church?

Try debriefing your kids on what they have just learned in Sunday School, Primary, priesthood, or Young Women. Or give the kids some ownership in this activity by having them ask the person next to them at the table what they learned. That will include you! Don't be too long-winded or philosophical, but tell them just enough to encourage other questions and comments. Thanking a child's teacher the next Sunday for a great lesson will be a surprise and a delight to the teacher as she/he realizes that what was taught actually went past the classroom door!

Church Jobs That Involve You More with Your Kids

Have you ever asked for a church job? It sounds a little improper, doesn't it, as well as a little dangerous!

Yet, if you do it the right way and for the right reason, it can sometimes prove to be a tremendously important step, and beneficial to all concerned.

We are not suggesting that you actually ask for a calling, but that you look for ward positions that would put you in direct contact with one or more of your kids, anything from Sunday School teacher to Scoutmaster (now there is one that the bishop would probably love a volunteer for). Mention to the bishop that you would be happy to volunteer or to help.

Do it with your eyes wide open, knowing that by volunteering, you may deprive your child of someone with more "social distance" who might teach him something you could not. But if you feel the need for the kind of contact a certain position could give you, as well as the desire to contribute to the other kids in that class or quorum or troop or team or whatever it is, then prayerfully consider talking about it with the bishop.

> ❦
>
> *You don't have to have the calling to help as a volunteer. You can be a driver for activities, a second person in two-deep leadership, or a substitute for a Sunday class.*
>
> ❦

Respecting his authority and inspiration, bring it up only as a possibility and tell the bishop that you would only want him to consider it if he felt impressed to do so. You don't have to have the calling to help as a volunteer. You can be a driver for activities, a second person in two-deep leadership, or a substitute for a Sunday class.

Upgraded Family Scripture Study

At almost every general conference I can remember since I was a little girl, families were urged over and over again to remember to read the scriptures together.

In trying our best to follow their advice when our kids were young, we tried to hold a brief devotional early in the morning every school day, which happened to be the only time we could squeeze it in with the other morning rituals and music practice that were required before school. It involved gathering in the living room with all the kids and reading a small section of scripture, usually from the Book of Mormon. There was a song and an opening and closing prayer. Sometimes the reading prompted some discussion but not usually . . . especially at that time of morning! We also talked about the issues of the day so that we could pray specifically for those who felt they needed extra help (see solution 3).

As a mom, I often wondered how much good we were really doing by just going through that rote process every morning, especially considering how many of the smaller children would drag their blankets up the stairs, settle in on a spot on the couch and be fast asleep after the first few verses, totally oblivious to what was going on. Our six-year-old daughter was the worst—no matter how many times we gently woke her up, she just couldn't keep her eyes open! Other children were in different stages of consciousness.

Imagine our delight when that same daughter pronounced years later as she was preparing for her mission to Romania that those morning scripture readings were some of her best memories! "But you were asleep most of the time you were there," I proclaimed.

"I know," she said, "but it was the good spirit I felt as I went to sleep and woke up that made me feel secure and happy to be part of a family who loved the scriptures and loved the Lord."

Our morning devotionals evolved over time, and the last ones occurred just before our last three children left home and also included our darling Bulgarian "daughter" Eva, who was brought home by our oldest daughter from her mission in Bulgaria to be part of our family. She attended college while living with us, and we had the privilege of sending her on her own mission. She even ended up marrying one of our dear friend's sons. She was a bit of sunshine added to those morning devotionals. By then there were no orders to "Wake up!" and less whining about "I have to finish my homework." And I must say that the discussions were much more stimulating.

In an effort to have everyone right on time, we met at six-five-four (6:54) and usually discussed just one of our favorite scriptures. Each person was assigned a day to bring a scripture that they loved or had found that week that had helped them in their daily struggles.

Family Home Evenings

What a blessing it is to have our wonderful Church leaders tell us again and again the importance of meeting with our families once a week. If we do it right, family home evenings help our kids to feel that our families are a living, working unit dedicated to helping and improving family members and to making a positive difference in the world. Through family home evenings our kids can feel they are part of something bigger than themselves, that their family is important and eternal, and that they are crucial members of a group of people bound together for eternity.

Of course, some of those Monday nights aren't quite as grand and glorious as that sounds. We often tell parents who have preschoolers that a fifteen-minute family home evening might be just fine. When there are older and younger children, it is a good idea to have a short meetings with a mini-lesson on the little kids' level at first and then excuse them to go play. The older children can then participate in family scheduling for the week and teach each other lessons about family values and join in the process of making family systems work better with their input.

As we speak and make parenting presentations to families outside of the Church, part of what we suggest is a strong recommendation for a weekly family meeting. This is a brand new idea to most parents, and they are often a little astounded that such a basic idea has just never occurred to them. We tell them that it is practiced by tens of thousands of families in our Church and that we guarantee positive results. Most of the families we speak to are strongly rooted in the business world, and when we ask them how they think their businesses would run without a staff and scheduling meeting each week they agree that it would soon lead to disaster. And when we suggest that their families are even more important than their businesses and need a meeting each week, maybe even more desperately than their businesses do to run smoothly, they all agree!

Still, with their busy lives, their first thought is often that they just couldn't be at a meeting once a week because they travel so much. We remind them that the same marvels of our electronics that help their businesses can also help their families. Conference calls and Skype are terrific ways to "be there" for their family at the family meeting each week. They become genuinely excited about the possibilities!

We give them ideas of how to do their meetings, including suggesting that, after the parents establish the routine, they let the kids have ownership of the meetings by letting them conduct and give a short lesson. If they are in need of material for a lesson, we direct them to www.familynightlessons.com, which gives them a nondenominational one-page lesson on a universal value that the kids can download and give themselves. Try it yourself if you are in need of a few new ideas.

One of the first things we often suggest they do in their family meetings is talk about a family mission statement similar to the one most of them have in their companies. We suggest that the best way to start is to have family members suggest individual words that describe the family as it should be or that suggest things that families should do. We tell them that the process of working on a family mission statement is even more important than the final product. In the end we tell them to keep it short, to boil it down to just a few words or two or three short thoughts.

We presented this to a group of families in Canada and then went back to the same group six months later to see how they were doing on our challenges. One cute mom came bouncing up to us and said, "Would you like to hear our family mission statement straight out of the minds of a six- and eight-year-old?"

"Sure," we said. Without missing a beat she said, "Here it is: Be thinkful, be thankful, and be BANANAS!" That family knew exactly what they were about, and their little kids wanted to be sure their mission statement had something about having fun in it.

The best family mission statements are highly spiritual and eternal in their scope. We know one family whose mantra is "return together" implying that they all wanted to return to the celestial kingdom. Another family's mission statement essentially says the same thing in different words: "No empty chairs."

We always held our family meetings around the dinner table which is where we established our family mission statement, talked about family laws and consequences for breaking those laws, set up a family economy, felt camaraderie, had arguments which sometimes included tears, anger, and stomping off, but where we also often felt the spirit of working together for the good of our family not only for now but for eternity.

Memorizing and Internalizing

Nothing brought about as much wailing and whining in our family as one of the kids who had just barely missed reaching some goal to which we had attached a reward. Because we are such pushovers, we found a way for kids to "make up" for what they had just missed or for what they finished after the deadline. That way was memorizing.

Memorizing a scripture or quote that embraced gospel principles (we had a list of favorites that they could choose from) was much more important than we realized at the time. Those scriptures and quotes, learned when they were children, are still a firm part of our children's memory banks and are still repeated often to their own children and at family gatherings. The sayings and verses are like old familiar friends. In hindsight it was more important than the rewards they received at the time or even than the satisfaction they got from committing something firmly to memory.

Sabbath Day

One thing no one would argue that the Church does for us is keep us busy on Sundays. It brings us together in a setting of worship and gives us a forum in which we teach each other the gospel.

But it also teaches us that the Sabbath is for more than going to Church.

There may be nothing more important to the spirituality and communication within a family than the full and joyful observance of the Sabbath day.

The busier and more hectic modern life gets, the more lovely it is to have the seventh day set aside to break the pace and provide a time to be more thoughtful, peaceful, and focused on the spiritual.

Sundays can also be the most pivotal and useful days for family togetherness and family communication.

> *Sundays can also be the most pivotal and useful days for family togetherness and family communication. Even bishops and Relief Society presidents can organize their time in such a way that they find some family time on Sunday afternoons or Sunday evenings.*

Of course Sundays are busy, particularly for those with heavy Church callings. But even bishops and Relief Society presidents can organize their time in such a way that they find some family time on Sunday afternoons or Sunday evenings.

Some families center their Sunday family time on what happens around the dinner table. In an effort to reward and give attention to positive behavior, we had four or five "weekly awards" that were always awarded to a child at Sunday dinner. One was the HUP award (Honesty under Pressure) that went to someone who had told the truth when it was hard. We would ask, "Who is in the running for the HUP award?"

and they would try to think of incidents during the past week that might qualify them.

Next was the SS award (Self Starter) that went to the child who had done the best job remembering his responsibilities and doing them without having to be reminded, or who saw needs and took action without being asked. Then there was the NAP (Neat as a Pin) Award for the one who had kept his room the cleanest, and finally, the biggest award, the WWJD (What Would Jesus Do?) that went to the child who could relate the best experience during the past week where he or she had asked that question to himself and done what he felt Jesus would have done.

The awards were nothing more than heavy construction paper with the initials written somewhat artistically on them. Kids would display them on their bedroom doors during the week until the next Sunday.

Scheduling for the week ahead was also done at the Sunday dinner table, with a big but simple family calendar where everyone could enter the events and things they had to get to during the week. There was a real motivation for this, since if something didn't get on the calendar, it might result in someone not getting picked up or dropped off. (We often ended the family scheduling feeling like we needed a chauffeur.)

The Age of Accountability

Consider for a moment the uniqueness and opportunity of the eight-to-twelve "window" in your children's growing years. During this unique phase of life, our children are highly conceptual and open to learning. They still think their parents are great (and that they know something). They are flattered by responsibility. They are not yet sarcastic or cynical, or at least not *much* that way yet.

The world calls it upper elementary age, or "preadolescence." We call it "the age of accountability." (Actually, that's what God calls it.)

Do we make enough of that insight? Do we appreciate this window and these teaching years, or do we "leave well enough alone" since this is the age when kids usually cause us the least amount of worries.

Too many parents do the latter. For evidence of that, visit the parenting section of a bookstore where you will find shelf after shelf of titles dealing with babies and preschoolers, and then even more shelves full of parenting books (and commiseration) about adolescents and teens. Where are the books about these "age of accountability" kids? Not there. Apparently parents take the attitude "if it ain't broke, don't fix it" or "let a sleeping dog lie"!

We feel that eight is the perfect age to talk to your child about sex. An eight-year-old is old enough to understand but not old enough to be cynical. And when parents start this early, they essentially make a "preemptive strike" and become the original source against which kids will bounce everything else they hear.

We saw the anxiety of so many parents over the years as they ap-

> *This short span between eight and twelve will never come again. That is when children are still sweet and naïve and impressionable, yet they are also conceptual, curious, and flattered by responsibility. And they still think you know what you are talking about!*

proached this topic, so we wrote a book simply called *How to Talk to Your Child about Sex*, which reads like a dialogue or a play. "You say this. . . . and your child will say this. Then you say this . . . and your child will say this, or this, in which case you say either this, or this . . ."

Parents liked it because it took the fear out of the discussion and approached the whole subject positively with the goal of helping kids avoid dangerous, early experimentation because they knew it would be much better if they waited for love, commitment, and marriage. The secondary goal, of course, is to help them have a healthy and beautiful physical intimacy within their marriage. The content of the book is now available at http://valuesparenting.com/talktokids.php.

Parents of kids at the age of accountability will know what we mean when we say that this is also the perfect age to start them tutoring younger children, babysitting responsibly, actively participating in family home evenings, earning and budgeting their own money, memorizing scriptures, and doing a host of other initiative-requiring things.

Also, think of the age of accountability as the magic window of time in which to prepare children to be responsible contributors in Young Women and Young Men activities and in priesthood quorums.

Remember, this short span between eight and twelve will never come again. That is when children are still sweet and naïve and impressionable, yet they are also conceptual, curious, and flattered by responsibility. And they still think you know what you are talking about! Take it while you can, parents!

Seminary and Institute

Have you ever told someone you were introduced to that you were a seminary graduate? Members of other faiths certainly do a double take, and look at you with a new appreciation or a new suspicion.

But think about it. What a wonder that our kids in the Church actually get a theology degree! In addition, the caliber of the seminary and institute lessons, the teachers, the assignments, and just spirituality in general has become even more stellar in recent years!

Those who were raised on the Wasatch Front have a whole new awakening of appreciation and of the blessings of released-time seminary when they move away or talk to other parents whose only option is the early morning variety. During the years we lived in McLean, Virginia, and our high school kids attended early morning seminary, we all learned a lot. What an incredible challenge! They were up at 5 A.M., ate breakfast, got ready for school, and had to be in their seats at the church, which was ten minutes away, by 6 A.M.

I have to admit that I'm an "owl" woman and not a "lark." Richard taught early morning seminary in Boston and again in Virginia, and I was usually still trying to sleep by the time he returned to get ready for work. My body timing wants to tell me to go to bed at midnight and get up at 7. Getting up at 5 A.M. is just not my idea of a good time! But get up we did when our own kids were in early morning seminary. And go to bed late we also did, because the schools they were attending in Fairfax County, Virginia, would rival any private school in scholastic demands. The homework was tough and enormously time-consuming. When our kids got to their first class at school, they had already been up for several hours, and they had had very little sleep the night before.

How we admire those great young people and their parents who carry on that schedule. And what amazing things they learn from doing something that hard for that long! One of our family mottos is "Hard Is Good." And it certainly is good for those valiant souls who love the Lord and who are obedient to their church leaders and parents who insist that they attend. Difficult times make for great stories and are part of that scaffolding that builds character as well as faith for the rest of their lives!

Missions

We don't take a lot of credit for the fact that all nine of our children have served missions. It happened largely because of the good circumstances and friends they had and also because our two oldest daughters, Saren and Shawni, made the decision to go and had such fabulous mission experiences in Bulgaria and Romania. They shared those experiences in weekly letters that we read to the younger children in family home evening.

Sometimes we are too close to the missionary system to have the full perspective of how wonderful it is. I recently sat by a chatty fellow on a plane who thought he knew quite a bit about The Church of Jesus Christ of Latter-day Saints, or the Mormon church, as he called it.

When he learned that I was a "high priest" in the Church, he began to tell me all his theories.

Among them was the idea that somewhere in those big buildings in Salt Lake, we had quite a group of psychologists and social scientists who, among other things, had come up with brilliant ideas for keeping old people from boredom, purposelessness, and isolation and for keeping young people out of trouble and giving them time to make good decisions about education, work, and family.

"Whoever came up with that temple thing was a genius," he said. "Imagine, a place where oldsters feel useful and important. And the missionary thing is even more brilliant. Kids at nineteen don't have a clue what they want to do, nor any real idea of the world around them, so you send them somewhere to learn a language or a culture and get out of their own selfish skin and mature enough to come home and make something of themselves—fantastic, just fantastic. Really, who came up with all that great stuff?"

Serving missions for The Church of Jesus Christ of Latter-day Saints is truly one of our modern-day miracles! Twenty-one-year-old young women and nineteen-year-old young men literally turn eighteen months to two years of their lives over to the Lord. Older couples also leave family and friends, miss births of grandchildren and family reunions, and forget themselves in the service of others. Mission presidents and their wives leave lucrative businesses, miss their children's weddings, and try to help with their grown children and grandchildren's health and financial problems from afar.

What makes missions so great is that they are so hard. We have often said that if people really knew how excruciatingly hard missions were, no one would go. But if people could know the joy that comes from actually changing people's lives through the gospel of Jesus Christ while putting themselves in a position to become more like Him in a life-changing way, no one would stay home!

Each of our children's mission experiences were different. Most had at least one difficult companionship, for a wide variety of reasons, and, of course, each mission president had his own style and approach. But all our missionary sons and daughters were able to follow the counsel that President Hinckley received from his father when he was a young missionary: "Forget yourself and go to work!"[2] In each case, their missions gave them a voice. The challenges of a mission helped them figure out who they really were and how to go forward with their future lives. Most of all, it gave them a firm testimony of our Heavenly Father's plan, a deep and abiding love for the Savior, and a determination to serve Him throughout their lives.

Because we have known Elder L. Tom Perry for so many years (he was Richard's stake mission president when he was a missionary in New York City and was our stake president in Boston), we have had the rare and special privilege of having his counsel and advice through the years. He has performed the marriages of many of our children, and when each child was contemplating a mission, he or she had a wonderful one-on-one conversation with him in his office.

When our number nine missionary, Charity, took her turn to talk about her decision to go on a mission, with a twinkle in his eye, Elder Perry said, "Because all your siblings have gone on missions, you must not have had much choice in the matter."

He told us that she shot back a quick and revealing response, "Oh yes, I had a choice, at least until I prayed about it. And then I got an answer, and I didn't have a choice anymore."

From the time children in the Church can barely talk, they hear the song "I Hope They Call Me on a Mission."[3] Faithful leaders, counselors, and bishops can talk to our growing children about missions until they are blue in the face, but a personal knowledge that a mission is right for them is the only reliable way to prepare for the inevitable hard times ahead.

Personal Stories of Prophets and
Family-Oriented Everyday Perspective

Besides their prophetic witnesses and warnings and guidance, I love our prophets for the family-centric examples they set. A couple of times those examples have been very close and personal.

Once, as a deacon in Logan, I was part of a priesthood outing to general conference. As fate would have it, we walked up to the west entrance to the tabernacle just as President McKay's car pulled up. While we boys watched with rapt attention from under the trees, two men helped the old and ailing prophet out of his seat in the back of the car, and then, to our amazement, he led (dragged) both of them around to the other side of the car where he opened the door and took the hand of his beloved Emma. As he helped her up out of the seat, with his two men still supporting him, he bent and kissed her and to my twelve-year-old brain that gesture and that kiss taught me about what mattered and about what it meant to be a man.

Many years later, the mission home phone rang in London and President Kimball's delightful secretary, Arthur Haycock, said, "President, I know this is short notice, but could you possibly meet the prophet's plane at Heathrow tomorrow night and get us to our London hotel for the night? We go on to France the next morning."

"Well, that's quite an imposition, you know," I joked with Arthur, "but I suppose I can manage it." I hung up the phone and sat there pondering the honor and wondering what I could do to express the love of the British saints to their prophet. An idea occurred to me, and I picked up the phone again, not taking as long to think about my impulse as I should have. I called Lord Grade, the film impresario and producer of movies such as *Chariots of Fire*, and with whom I had become acquainted. I asked him for the loan of his limo. "I want to make our elderly president comfortable," I explained, "and our mission van is anything but."

"Sure," he said, "Which limo would you like me to send?"

Which limo? Now I started to realize that maybe this was not the best idea.

"Never mind," he said. "I'll send a nice one. What time?"

The next evening, sitting in the den in the front of the mission home, I thought momentarily that we were experiencing an eclipse. It suddenly grew dark. I looked up, and what was blocking the sun was the largest, longest car I had ever seen. The enormous Rolls Royce was longer than the width of the mission home, and at this point, all I could do was go out and jump in with the uniformed, capped driver.

All the way to the airport I thought about the inappropriateness of this. President Kimball— the humblest and smallest of prophets, quiet, dignified and unassuming—was about to be picked up in a monstrous Rolls Royce. Would he jokingly ask me for a look at the mission budget or would he dip an eyebrow and wonder just what was going on here?

> ⌘
>
> *What President Kimball cared about was a person, a young man, probably a father, out late because of him. What he cared about was a little family waiting for their dad. What he cared about was what mattered.*
>
> ⌘

He did neither, of course. He was tired, his plane was late, and with a gracious smile, he simply walked with Arthur and me to the waiting car and climbed in. He had to walk awhile to get to the backseat, and I climbed in the front with the young, uniformed chauffeur.

About halfway to London on the dark motorway, I heard President Kimball get up and walk up toward me. *Here comes the question about the mission budget*, I thought. But it was the chauffeur he was headed for. He put his hand on his shoulder and said, "Young man, I'm so sorry our plane was late and you have to be out at this hour. We are probably keeping you from your family."

I had a little time to ponder as we continued down the road. It was another example I will never forget. This very old, very tired man did not think or care about the car or the comfort or the appearance or the status (or even about the mission budget). What he cared about was a person, a young man, probably a father, out late because of him. What he cared about was a little family waiting for their dad. What he cared about was what mattered.

IMPACTS

What It Helps Us Bring to Pass

The powerful backup and support that the Church gives parents can be the difference between success and failure in many different areas. But the fact that it is *there* and *available* is not enough. If we fully avail ourselves and our kids to the programs of the Church, and if we apply the ongoing and always current advice of present-day Church leaders, it becomes vastly more likely that we can bring certain incredibly valuable things to pass.

Better speaking and communication skills. It is amazing what the Church and its programs do for our kids in these areas.

Empathy, caring, sharing, and working with others. Within the organization and activities of the Church, our children learn to forget themselves and serve.

Great friends. Peers can make or break a child, and the Church gives our kids a cadre of reliable friends.

Backup, support, and mentors. Parents get the backup they need on the values and truths they teach, and kids get advisors and mentors who can last a lifetime.

Spiritual knowledge as a defense. Constant learning in the

Church arms children with testimony and the ability to recognize and withstand error.

Family unity via shared beliefs, practices, and worship. Church activity together creates quality time and bonding.

Examples. Everyone needs models, and kids who are active will find worthy individuals that they want to emulate.

What It Helps Us Avoid or Overcome

An accurate description for much of God's ancient counsel and for the current counsel we receive at General Conference and via other messages of our prophets is "a voice of warning." By paying attention, and by strong activity in Church programs, there are many problems that can be avoided or that can be escaped.

Growing up too fast. The rules, standards, and norms of the Church essentially retard social growth and keep kids from things they are not yet ready for.

ADHD and other mental and emotional disorders. While not a cure-all, and while professional help is also often needed, the Church gives a structure and a focus that often helps in these areas.

Guilt. Church and priesthood interviews help members resolve past mistakes, clear the air, and nip problems in the bud.

Selfishness. The occupied, serving mind of a child in the Church leaves less room to think and worry about self.

Too much time texting and online. Church activity is a great take-over from "cyberactivity."

Worldly mind-sets. Spiritual and family-oriented thinking, so common in Church settings and activity, can push aside worldly perspectives.

Aimlessness. The structure and timetables of missions, temple marriage, and other Church goals can provide a framework for progress and purpose.

SOLUTION

5

Remember the Savior's Power

Use His Spirit to guide, His Atonement to save, and His Priesthood to bless our children. *Put simply, the responsibility for others of God's children is more than we can handle on our own, and giving us that responsibility is too big a risk for God to take. So . . . He does give us the stewardship . . . but He also surrounds us with supernal help: The Light of Christ, the power of the priesthood, the gift of His Holy Spirit, and the redeeming, saving power of the Atonement.*

If you were going to send your child into the care of surrogate parents for a period of time, would you not want to give that person all of the help you could to take care of your child? You might give them the keys to your car, the directions to get the child to wherever he needed to go, and you would give as much information as you could about your child and his needs.

And you would give them power of authority—to discipline, to instruct, to sign papers, to talk to teachers, or to do whatever else the child would need while the child was gone from you.

Heavenly Father gives all that and more to us, His stewards and the surrogate parents of His children.

He gives us His power to bless them! He gives us guidance from His Spirit, and He gave us all His only Begotten Son to save us.

The fifth spiritual solution is to *remember* the gifts that our Savior has given us to build our foundation on them and our lives around them. Although the scriptures are full of the "unsearchable riches of Christ" (Ephesians 3:8) our favorite reference is found in Helaman 5:12: "And now, my sons [and daughters], remember, remember that it is upon the rock of our Redeemer, who is Christ, the Son of God, that ye must build your foundation; that when the devil shall send forth his mighty winds, yea, his shafts in the whirlwind, yea, when all his hail and his mighty storm shall beat upon you, it shall have no power over you to drag you down to the gulf of misery and endless wo, because of the rock upon which ye are built, which is a sure foundation, a foundation whereon if men build they cannot fall."

I especially love the symbolism of the "shafts in the whirlwind." We have all encountered them as mothers. I always think of an Olympic torch flying through a hurricane and hitting me directly in the head, which seems to symbolically happen quite often as we raise our children. Besides the whirlwinds, it seems that there is always one of Satan's imps, as described in *The Screwtape Letters* by C. S. Lewis,[1] who is sitting on our shoulder telling us to do things that will create mighty storms in our lives that could drag us down to misery and endless woe. Yet, if we are built upon the rock of our Savior, those storms will have no power over us. What a lesson for our children to learn and remember!

As much as I love the Savior, I know mothers of other faiths who put me to shame when it comes to having the Savior always at the conscious center of their lives. He is their first thought in the morning and their last thought at night. It is as though they have frontlets that the orthodox Jews wear. The frontlet is a leather strap worn around the forehead to which little boxes are attached. Passages of scripture written on parchment are placed inside to be a constant reminder.

Wouldn't it be great if we had our own frontlets on our foreheads with that scripture and/or other favorites to remind us of the importance of the Savior's sacrifice and example? With those thoughts always dangling before our eyes, it seems that it would be a lot easier to always remember Him as we promise we will do each week when we partake of the sacrament.

INSIGHTS

The Faith of Little Children

I remember so clearly an incident from my own boyhood. I had contracted a serious ear infection, and the right side of my head had swelled up like a balloon. The doctor couldn't seem to find an antibiotic that would work, and everyone was getting alarmed. I was six, and all I know was that it hurt—bad!

I guess someone had taught me about priesthood blessings, because I wanted one and wondered why we hadn't done it sooner. Why had I been hurting and throbbing like this for days instead of just fixing it with the priesthood? My dad anointed, and my Grandfather Swenson gave me the blessing. I heard the words "better" and "cure" in there somewhere, and that was enough for me.

When it was done, I remember standing up from the chair, looking up at my grandfather and asking, "Will it be better today or will it take until tomorrow?"

Kids have faith. It is a natural kind of faith. In fact it is as natural as wanting to eat, as natural as believing in their parents, as natural as believing in their Heavenly Father. Clearly, one of the things Christ meant when He told us to be as little children was to have childlike faith.

"Use the Priesthood More Often"

We were at a fireside one night in Cambridge, Massachusetts, and the speaker, a wonderful Church leader, had opened the meeting to questions on any subject. The audience was composed mostly of married graduate students and professors from the area—Harvard, MIT, Boston University, Tufts—an intellectual group.

One graduate student, a young father, raised his hand and asked, "How can I have more spiritual experiences? I had them all the time on my mission!"

The Church leader gave him a rather short answer: "Use the priesthood more."

"What exactly do you mean?" the student followed up.

"Just use the priesthood more."

The meeting and the questions and answers went on, and the student kept his hand in the air.

Finally the Church leader called on him again and he said, "I'm sorry, but I just don't quite know what you mean by 'use the priesthood more.'"

This time the speaker elaborated. He told us that every time we used the priesthood of God in our home, to bless our wives, to bless a child, even to bless our home itself, we would have a spiritual experience. Then he said one last line that I have always remembered. "I don't think I have ever met anyone who uses the priesthood too much."

The priesthood is the key to strong families. Even when you are not giving an actual blessing, think of yourself as a priesthood holder. Feel and magnify the priesthood when you pray, when you teach, when you discipline, when you comfort. Use it in the way you live. And women should share their husband's priesthood. It is the power of your family. Think of yourself as part of it and feel it in your life and in how you raise your children and in how you pray about your children.

We need to teach our children to ask for blessings when they need them and to think of the priesthood as a part of family life, as a great and wonderful tool that Heavenly Father has given us to bring spiritual solutions into our home. Obviously, blessings should not be given for frivolous things, but when there is a real concern, a genuine worry or need, maybe even on something that an adult might think of as a small matter, a priesthood blessing can be given.

Who Might Need a Priesthood Blessing?

- A young daughter worried about an upcoming test, almost to a point of feeling physically ill
- A son with a big game coming up
- A wife with more than she can handle in the week ahead with her mother visiting and the book club meeting at her home
- A little boy having a hard time learning to read
- A little girl devastated by a fight with her best friend who is now "not speaking"
- A son being bullied at school
- A daughter who is not eating well and may be on the verge of an eating disorder
- A twelve-year-old troubled by an inappropriate movie he saw at a friend's house
- A girl worried about starting junior high
- A high school son preparing to take the SAT or the ACT

Of course you don't bless the daughter with an "A" or the son with twenty points in the basketball game, but you follow the Spirit and bless them with a focused mind or a confidence to do their best. Often, within the blessing itself, there will come an answer or a prompting of an action or a way they can do more to bless themselves and to better realize their own desires.

"Handing the Phone to God"

We have a friend who has an interesting perspective on performing priesthood blessings. "It's one thing to talk about God," he says, "which we do in Church classes and in devotionals and in family home evenings. It's a whole other thing to actually talk *to* Him in prayer. But a priesthood blessing is like someone handed the telephone to God so that He can speak directly to us in His own voice."

Using the priesthood more often causes us to become better at being the voice for His words, and better at feeling the Spirit and saying what God wants us to say.

Learning from Other Christians

Of course it's not only about using the Lord's priesthood; it's about emulating His life and loving His example and trying to follow it.

As we speak to (and speak with) Christians of other denominations, we are often amazed at how Christ-centered they are in their everyday lives and in their parenting.

If we are not careful in the Church, the abundance of additional insights that come with the restored gospel can give us so much to think about that it may dilute how much we think about Christ. As wonderful as the plan of salvation or the Word of Wisdom or the ward and stake activities might be, we should be on guard against filling our minds with them so much that there is little room to focus on the center of it all, which is Christ.

Some of our Christian friends—who don't have the full restored gospel of Jesus Christ with all its additional knowledge—focus solely on Christ, because He is the sum total of what they know.

And it is wonderful to behold. They ask themselves often "What would Jesus do?" and then they do it.

APPLICATIONS

Ways to Use the Priesthood in Every LDS Home

Giving priesthood blessings in the home is such a powerful tool in raising our children. And a blessing can be performed whenever a child asks for one or there seems to be an appropriate need.

Some two-parent, two-member families have a tradition that the mother, who shares the priesthood with her husband, offers an opening prayer before blessings are performed, asking for the Spirit to influence her husband as he gives the blessing, and to inspire him to say the words the Lord would want said.

There are many faithful LDS families where the priesthood does not reside—those of single women, single mothers with young children, widows, or families where the father is not a member or doesn't hold the priesthood. In those cases, it is at least as important and may be even more important to ask for blessings. Home teachers are usually delighted to give blessings. Bishops can fill in as necessary. No one in the Church is without access to this great power and to the opportunity to have it used in direct blessings on their heads.

We recently spoke at a fireside especially for widows. Most were in their thirties and forties and had lost spouses in almost every imaginable way. During the course of the evening, we learned more about the gospel from their amazing examples of faith and perseverance than any little thing we could have taught them! They spoke of being surrounded by the priesthood power through their trials and of what stability it gave to them and their families.

We also speak frequently to single members over thirty and have been amazed at their faith and appropriate reliance on the priesthood. In all, no matter what your age or family situation, remembering that the Savior's power comes in large part through priesthood ordinances is one of the best things we can do to bring more spirituality to our homes.

Annual School Year Blessings

At the advice of a good mentor, we began the practice of giving a "school year blessing" to each of our children at the beginning of school each fall. It was a serious and anticipated occasion, held on the Sunday preceding the first day of school, in the living room with all kids in attendance and the phones turned off.

As a mother, I learned so much from those blessings. Richard said what he felt from the Spirit to each child, and there were insights that neither of us had thought of before. We usually spent a little time the evening prior to the blessings talking together as a couple about the needs and the gifts of each child and praying together that the blessings would be in accordance with the Lord's will for each one of our children. And we would also ask the kids to mention to their dad anything they were worried about when school started and anything they thought they might need special help with during the year ahead. Those who had already set some school-year goals were invited to share them before their blessings.

The children took notes, writing down all they could remember right after the blessing, and their notes became a further input and guide to their school-year goals.

Looking back, there is no question in my mind that many, many of the promises of those blessings were fulfilled, and perhaps of equal importance, I think each of the children approached their school year with more of a spiritual perspective and with the feeling that they could pray about both their goals and their challenges. They saw how seriously we took blessings, prayer, and the priesthood, and it seemed to rub off on them.

A Mother's Birthday Prayer

We know one family that has another "spiritual event" on an annual basis for each of their children. On the morning of a child's birthday, the family gathers for their "devotional" just before breakfast and the mother offers a special birthday prayer. In it she expresses gratitude for the child and all of his or her great qualities and for the contributions the child makes to the family.

Then she asks in faith, and accompanied by the faith of the rest of the family, for the blessings she feels the birthday child is in need of.

We have often thought how appropriate it would be to combine an annual "mother's prayer" each year on a child's birthday with a "father's blessing" on the first day of school, giving a child two times each year when the family's spiritual faith and thought are focused just on him or her and when blessings are called down for the year ahead.

Blessings before Trips

I had to travel extensively with my business while our children were small, and I worried about them, and about Linda at home without me, trying to care for all their needs.

We began a practice of giving the children a collective priesthood blessing each time before I left on a trip. We would gather on the couch, positioning Linda beside me and all the children clustered on or behind the couch, and each touching me while I gave them a blessing of safety and well-being while I was away.

We have no warmer memory than of those blessings, all of us in physical contact with each other, and the spirit and power of the priesthood flowing through us, feeling one another's love and feeling how dependent we all were on Heavenly Father and on His ability to bless us and keep us well and safe.

Seeking and Following the Spirit

We should understand as parents that there is no greater blessing for kids or help for parents than the presence of the Holy Ghost. We have so many potential opportunities to ask for and to attract the Spirit.

We used to have a car with a very sensitive but somewhat erratic radio. It was predigital and it would pick up all kinds of signals, but it had the old turning knob station selector, and unless you got it exactly on the station there was a lot of static and fade-out. And even when you got good reception, it would fade gradually and you would have to tune it in all over again.

The Spirit seems to operate similarly. We need to work at staying tuned in, and when we do, the rewards are truly remarkable. We become calm and clear, and we understand people and situations in a sensitive way. And best of all, as mentioned earlier, the feelings and calmness are contagious to our children.

Parley P. Pratt, in his classic little book *Key to the Science of Theology*, described the effects that the Holy Ghost can have on our natures:

"The gift of the Holy Ghost adapts itself to all [our] organs or attributes. It quickens all the intellectual faculties, increases, enlarges, expands, and purifies all the natural passions and affections, and adapts them, by the gift of wisdom, to their lawful use. It inspires, develops, cultivates, and matures all the fine-toned sympathies, joys, tastes, kindred feelings, and affections of our nature. It inspires virtue, kindness, goodness, tenderness, gentleness, and charity. It develops beauty of person, form, and features. It tends to health, vigor, animation, and social feeling. It invigorates all the faculties of the physical and intellectual man."[2]

It is a good idea to make a request for the Spirit to be with us as part of every family prayer. Identify the Spirit whenever you feel it so that children can become more and more familiar with what the Holy Ghost feels like and can ask for Him in their own lives. One of our daughters has done such a good job with this that her little four-year-old, Charlie, says, even in his blessings on the food, "Help us to feel the Holy Spirit."

Some of our own children remember very clearly some of the efforts we made to try to help them, at very young ages, understand how the Holy Ghost feels. We would do things like putting a piece of sandpaper in the freezer for a while and then asking a little kid to feel it and describe how it felt. "Cold and rough," they would say. Then we would have them feel a soft blanket just out of the dryer, and they would respond, "Warm and soft."

"Which one feels most like the Holy Ghost?" we would ask.

Part of the fasting and testimony-bearing experience within a family should be to help children to recognize the feeling of the Spirit. Older kids will respond well to descriptive discussions involving words like calm, peaceful, warm, soft, clear, and light.

> *Identify the Spirit whenever you feel it so that children can become more and more familiar with what the Holy Ghost feels like and can ask for Him in their own lives.*

Whatever we can do to make the Spirit seem real and accessible to our children is worth the time and effort it takes.

The Sacrament

Of course, when it comes to "remembering" the Savior, there is no greater or more consistent approach than the ordinance God has established for that very purpose, the sacrament of the Lord's Supper.

We know that the prime reason we have sacrament meeting, and the most important reason for attending, is to partake of the sacrament and to renew our covenants of baptism, which are to always remember Jesus Christ, to keep His commandments, and to take upon us His name.

We should try hard to help our children, even at a young age, be aware of these three promises that we make to God every Sunday, and of the return promise He makes us, that we may always have His Spirit to be with us.

There is no better recurring discussion to have at the Sunday dinner table than one about the sacrament. Depending on the age of your children, start with basic questions that get them involved and build on what they know.

What Do We Know About the Sacrament?
- What does the bread represent? What about the water?
- What are the promises we make when we take the sacrament?
- Have we made these promises before? (If they have been baptized)
- What does it mean to "take upon us His name"?
- What does it mean to "always remember Him"?
- What does it mean to "keep His commandments which He has given us"?

We are always interested in the methods various families use to try to keep their children focused on the sacrament while it is being passed. Some have pictures of Jesus or books about Jesus for their small children to look at during the sacrament. Others keep the Cheerios and the quiet toys and books hidden away until after the sacrament. Still others ask their children to write down one thing they love about Jesus while the bread is being passed, and another thing during the water.

Families with older children sometimes focus on one aspect of the Savior to think about during the sacrament each week. A guide for doing this, with a separate facet of Christ's personality or character outlined for focus each week of the year, can be found at www.WhatMannerOfMan .com. This guide is taken from a volume we wrote for our missionaries in England to assist them in keeping their minds on the Lord during the partaking of the sacrament and to expand their view of who the Savior was and is and of His personal qualities that we can emulate.

At a stage when most of our kids were still home and we were dealing with three preschoolers and a plethora of kids all along our church bench, I remember regretting that all my time during the sacrament seemed to be spent trying to keep the little kids from talking out loud and fighting over the "sacrament book" I had brought to calm them down. Having spent an evening with Truman and Ann Madsen about that time, I asked Ann what she did to calm her children during the sacrament and help them feel the gravity of the ordinance they were participating in.

The answer she gave was something I have used for many years. She said something like this: "Sit by a different child each week and in between preschool outbursts put your arm around that child and whisper these thoughts:

"Do you know that this is the most special moment of the week? For just a short few minutes we get to really think hard about our love for Jesus and how He gave His life for us. You get to take upon yourself His name for the whole rest of the week which means you can try to think of things to do that would please Jesus. You can try to think of someone you can help this week. That would make Jesus happy."

Kids from about five on up through teenagers responded well to this. I didn't get around to each child very often but when I did, it gave them a good reminder of what the sacrament is really about!

Creating a Spiritual Atmosphere in Your Home

We've tried everything on this one, including, as mentioned earlier, leaving the Christmas tree up until March since it seemed to generate a certain calm in our home. Do anything you can do to make the home feel a little like a sanctuary and a safe and spiritual place. We've even tried dimming the lights, whispering, and various kinds of meditation, but perhaps the best method for creating a warmer, softer feeling in the home is music.

As a musician and a mom who loves music, nothing seems to bring the Spirit more quickly or more surely than having classical music playing. I know, to each his own. Different people are moved by different things. Whether it is a country western song by George Strait that speaks to your soul, a Yo-Yo Ma rendition of an unaccompanied Suite by J. S. Bach, Louis Armstrong singing "It's a Wonderful World," or even Diana Krall singing soft jazz, music can change your mood. You can take it one step higher to truly spiritual music; a Mack Wilberg arrangement of "Come, Thou Fount of Every Blessing" sung by the Mormon Tabernacle Choir can lift your soul and help you feel the Spirit enough to almost reach out and touch it!

The Calming, Spirit-Bringing Power of Spiritual Music

Every summer I have what I call "Grammie Camp" just before or just after our family reunions in July. It gives me a chance to get to know our grandchildren a few at a time. I take them in batches, and the youngest group that gets to go to Grammie Camp is the rambunctious five to eight-year-olds.

It just lasts one day, but we pack a lot in. We start in the evening and have a "sleepover" together. We begin with lessons on ancestors followed with Swedish Fish rewards (I rationalize them because many of our forebearers are Swedish) for those who can remember the names on both sides of the family for three generations. The next morning we learn a Grammie Camp song and a special quote or scripture for the year. Because our ancestors valued work so much we also include a little work. There are always plenty of weeds to pull!

This year was the first year for our little five-year-old identical twins, Oliver and Silas, to attend, and they were as excited as sixteen-year-olds going to their first school dance.

After the twins had sat attentively for a while on the first evening, they got a little restless and started literally jumping off the walls. Instead of reprimanding them for being a bit too wild, I put on a CD of Jenny Oaks Baker playing a wonderful arrangement of "Jesus Once Was a Little Child." Without any prompting and within two minutes they became calm. The little girls started dancing gracefully and the boys joined in. Although they may not have realized it, the music was a powerful prompter for peace and a feeling of quiet tranquility.

Spiritual music played on Sundays has such an amazing ability to bring the spirit to the Sabbath, and if you are like us, you may need a dose of it occasionally on weekdays too!

God's House and Your House

D&C 88:119 talks about establishing a house, "even a house of prayer, a house of fasting, a house of faith, a house of learning, a house of glory, a house of order, a house of God." It is speaking, of course, about the temple, about God's house, but it applies so perfectly to our houses, to the homes we want to establish for our children. Clearly, making our houses more like God's house is a worthy goal.

Early in our marriage, Linda, who has always loved to paint, got a big canvas and painted on it an artistic rendition of the words from that verse. That painting has had a place in our home for decades now, and still reminds us of the similarities we can try to create between our houses and God's house.

The temple, of course, is the great symbol of all that we believe about the eternal family. It is a useful exercise, occasionally as we go to temple sessions, to listen to the ceremony with family foremost in mind. Ask yourself with every phrase and every symbol, "What does this teach me about family?"

You will find that eternal family is the theme of almost all that you hear and do in the temple.

Scripture and Testimonies as Gauges and Measures

Elder Bednar, in an extremely interesting conference talk in April 2010, told us that reading scriptures and bearing testimony was a good way to measure or gauge the spiritual well-being of our children. When a child is reading a scripture or bearing his or her testimony, it is often easy to see beneath the words and get a feeling of how this stewardship of ours is doing deep within his or her soul.[3]

Monthly Family Testimony Meetings

Family testimony meetings not only let us gauge our children's spiritual well-being, they are also the surest way to bring the Spirit into our homes.

> *One single thing that has contributed most to the spirituality of our children, and to the strength of their testimonies, would probably be our monthly family testimony meeting.*

In fact, as a mom, if I had to pick one single thing that has contributed most to the spirituality of our children, and to the strength of their testimonies, it would probably be our monthly family testimony meeting. Someone gave us this idea years ago and it has served us so well for so long!

Every fast Sunday after our meetings and just before breaking our fast, we all gather in the living room for a short testimony meeting with our kids. I don't mind admitting that the children over eight who were fasting all agreed that we should break our fast *fast* after our meetings, but even though we all went into the family testimony meetings starving, we all left feeling well-fed. Even our three-year-olds reached a point where they wanted to say something.

As we began our meetings we carefully coached the small children, telling them that we loved hearing them express their love for each other, and couldn't wait to hear them share any spiritual experiences they had that week. But the most important thing to say before they finished their testimony was to say how they felt about the Savior.

Since the Church now strongly encourages children to bear their testimonies in Primary and in the home, rather than in Sacrament Meeting, our family testimony meeting might have been ahead of its time. The simple fact is that the bearing of testimony draws the Spirit, and family testimonies are no exception. In fact, there may be no place more appropriate for the sharing of feelings and faith than within the eternal unit of family.

When families start the tradition of a family testimony meeting on fast Sunday in the time between coming home from Church and having the Sunday meal, it is not always a slam dunk or an instant success. Kids often can't think of anything to say and don't automatically or instantly warm to the idea.

What we have found though, is that if parents explain it well, and treat it as a very grown-up thing to do that they now think their kids are old enough for, (and if they don't expect too much at first—just a simple expression of what a child loves is a good start), then the testimonies become better each month and kids gradually start to look forward to them.

As they became more comfortable with bearing their testimonies, we heard some truly incredible stories and there was a lot of love flowing in that room by the end of the meeting each month.

Stories emerged in children's testimonies that we would otherwise never have heard . . . about helping other kids who were being bullied or attempts to include certain girls in their "groups" when others were trying to exclude them.

Establishing a family testimony meeting every fast Sunday may not be an easy thing to do, especially if you start when your kids are teenagers, but the more practice they get at home, the easier it will be for them to bear their testimonies as they grow up. It is our belief that kids don't really know how they feel until they verbalize it!

We started our family testimony meeting ritual while we were on our mission in England. I'm sure being immersed in a spiritual atmosphere made it a lot easier. Saren, the oldest of our four children at the time, was five when we arrived and eight when we returned. She was a valiant oldest child with a strong spirit that made it so much easier as the younger children looked to her example.

When I think about our family testimonies in London, I think about a certain living room couch in the mission home where we all sat for those meetings. When we first arrived in England, I thought this particular couch was the ugliest thing I had ever seen. *How can I live with this couch for three years?* I thought! By the time we came home, we had gathered around that couch for testimony meetings every month for three years, not only with our family but with our amazing missionaries, and I found that I wanted to take that beautiful couch home with me! I loved what it reminded me of and what we had learned and felt as we had assembled around it and shared the feelings of our hearts.

Once we were home from our mission and had our own children going into the mission field, we established a ritual of sending each family member's handwritten testimonies which were to be read by the missionary on Christmas morning. Here is the testimony our eight-year-old Charity sent one year. As you will see, the spelling is intact and is not her forte!

> "I know the gospl is true, that Jesus lives and I know that the articals of faith are good and tell about the true church (this one). I love the prophet and all my nighbors. That means I love everyone, even if there strangers, robors and so on. I just don't like the things they do. I love you Elder Eyre!"

Christ-Centered Lives

A dear friend told us of a lake community where his and a number of other families who were members of the Church have been spending their summer vacations for many decades.

As he has observed the various families over many years, all active, committed Church families, he began to put them in three categories:

• Some were predominantly family-centered, and they focused most of their attention on the importance and strength of their family.

• Some were predominantly Church-centered, and they talked and oriented everything to being active and engaged in the church.

• Some were predominantly Christ-centered, and they seemed to put the Savior at the top of their consciousness and their conversation.

As the years went by, our friend said, and as children grew up and had careers and families of their own, rifts and rivalries—and in some cases, individuals leaving the faith or family members not wanting to come to reunions or gatherings anymore—developed in the family-centered and church-centered families, but *not* in the Christ-centered families.

Of course we should be family-centric and church-centric in our families, but unless there is an even higher level of prime focus, namely the Savior himself, we will never find the full unity and love that is spiritually available to us all.

The Motivation of the Atonement

Was it necessary for God to sacrifice His beloved son for our sins to be removed? Could there conceivably have been another way? Couldn't God, in His omnipotence, simply have wiped our slates clean without sending His Only Begotten Son into such agony?

It is a question far too deep for these pages, but what is certain is that no other method of atonement would have provided the motivation that Christ's Atonement does. As we grow to love Him, and to stand in awe of what He did for us (which two things seem to happen in tandem), there is a tug toward righteousness and a sorrow for sin that could not be duplicated in any other way.

We often assume that the Atonement is impossible for children to comprehend. After all, we know that we cannot fully grasp it ourselves.

C. S. Lewis wanted so badly to share his convictions of the Atonement with all, particularly with children, and it led him to write the classic book in the Chronicles of Narnia series called *The Lion, the Witch, and the Wardrobe*,[4] in which the great lion Aslan saves the children from the clutches of the White Witch. Our favorite parts of the book are the two culminating chapters. The first is titled "Deep Magic from the Dawn of Time." In it, because of the mistakes of the boy Edmund, the White Witch claims him for her own through the rule of justice.

The next chapter is called "Deeper Magic from before the Dawn of Time." In it, the magnificent Aslan employs the even higher law of mercy and redeems and saves the boy by sacrificing himself, and then to the awe and amazement of all, Aslan comes back to life.

Did C. S. Lewis know of the premortal life before the dawn of mortality where the "deeper magic" of the plan of justice and mercy and the Atonement were revealed?

He certainly knew of and had a powerful belief in the Atonement, and his writings are the best way we have ever found to begin to help young children grasp the power of what Christ did for us.

Les Misérables by Victor Hugo[5] is another powerful story about justice and mercy and the ultimate triumph of the latter over the former. It is a story all of our children should experience sometime in their teen years, either in the book, or on stage, or as a movie.

The Model of Christ

Sometimes the best way to keep something in the conscious mind is simply to be looking at it all the time. Along with the music and sports posters that adorned our children's rooms, we managed to find a central place in each room reserved for a picture of the Savior. Over the years we had found nine different paintings that we loved, and those nine framed pictures adorned the walls of each of our children's rooms for many years. Part of our Sunday activities was that each child would bring his picture to the dinner table, and the prints would rotate one person to the right, so that each child had a different rendition of the Savior each week, and so that each of the paintings spent a week with each of our children every ninth week.

IMPACTS

Of course, the priesthood, the Atonement, and the Spirit can impact *every* part of our lives and our children's lives, but it is good to review some examples of things these spiritual forces can help us bring to pass and of things we can strive to avoid or overcome.

What They Help Us Bring to Pass

Receptivity to the Gift of the Holy Ghost and the worship and emulation of the Savior can be manifest in our use of the priesthood to bless our children. That powerful combination can bring some enormously important things to pass.

More sharing and serving. The more our children feel the Spirit and ask the "What Would Jesus Do?" question, the more attuned they become to the needs of others.

Stronger testimonies. All of the methods discussed to make Christ more real and the Spirit more strong will contribute to our children's testimonies.

Getting along with others. Bickering and competition lessen in a spiritual atmosphere, and cooperation grows.

Supernal help. Priesthood blessings call down power vastly beyond our own and apply it to the things worrying or plaguing our children.

Sanctuary. The spiritual atmosphere we create in our homes can seem like a safe harbor from the criticism and cynicism and pressure of the outside world.

Motivation. Nothing motivates what a child wants to do or to be as much as a basic understanding of the Atonement and of how much Christ has done to give us this life of self-determination.

"His Spirit to be with us." If our children keep the attending challenges of remembering Him, following Him, and taking His name, they will have His Spirit with them.

What They Help Us Avoid or Overcome

In the course of father's priesthood blessings, we are often made spiritually aware of dangers or temptations our children are or will be facing, and we can bless them in specific ways that will help them move away from perilous situations. There are a whole host of problems that a watchful, prayerful parent may be able to avoid or to nip in the bud, and while appropriate medical and professional help should always be sought if and when serious problems manifest, there are none that are not also subject to the power of prayer and priesthood.

ADHD and eating disorders. These problems are too tough to confront alone, and spiritual help as well as professional help is called for.

Drugs and alcohol. Kids who learn what a spiritual high feels like will desire a chemical one less.

Pornography. Titillation and the addiction of pornography simply can't survive in a spiritual atmosphere (or a spirit-influenced mind).

Violence. Any kind of coarseness or dangerous or degrading activity or experience has little appeal to a mind that is oriented to spiritual things.

Depression. Again the combination of medical and spiritual help should be sought. As Paul taught, "For God hath not given us the spirit of fear; but of power, and of love, and of a sound mind" (2 Timothy 1:7).

Insecurity and loneliness. Children who have come to think of Christ and of the Spirit as real will rarely feel inadequate or alone.

Being blindsided as parents. Listening to our children's testimonies and scripture reading and other spiritual activity can be an early warning signal that tips parents off about alienation or other problems that may be developing.

CONCLUSION

Spiritual solutions!

The most amazing thing about them is that the Spirit will bring them into our minds. Parents who view their children (and themselves) as spiritual beings having a mortal experience will increasingly find that, no matter how "worldly" the problem, there is a spiritual solution that can help.

This book has certainly not mentioned or even hinted at them all, but it has tried to suggest enough spiritual solutions that a spiritual reader will shift paradigms a bit and begin to find more of them in everyday living.

There will still be frustrations, still be problems, and still be days when we are completely overwhelmed, but as we remember who our children really are, as we follow God's own parenting patterns, as we pray as stewards and surrogate parents, and as we fully use the Church, the gospel, the Spirit, and the priesthood, we can move to a new and higher level in the greatest calling we have, and the one calling that will never end.

EXECUTIVE SUMMARY

The following is a brief summary of the main ideas that we have presented in each chapter and may prove helpful in trying to locate a particular idea or story.

Perspectives: Worldly Challenges, Spiritual Solutions

Parents all over the world face similar and escalating challenges in this age of materialism, entitlement, and amorality. The restored gospel gives us insightful access to spiritual solutions, if we can only remember them and apply them.

Solution 1: Remember Your Children's True Identity

Apply what we know about where our children came from and discover their unique eternal personalities.

Understanding that our children are actually our spiritual siblings causes us to respect them as well as love them. What an advantage to know that "they are who they are." We didn't create them. Each is a unique spiritual personality and not just a reflection of who *we* are or who we want them to be. We can apply this knowledge to issues of self-esteem, peer pressure, bullying, development of talent and potential, sibling rivalry, safety, insecurity, and more. Ideas from this chapter include the following:

- Identifying practical ways to extend and receive spiritual respect
- Apologizing to children
- Learning to know kids individually; accurately recognizing unique gifts and challenges
- Helping your children know more about their spiritual selves

- Getting rid of guilt and understanding that you are not "starting from scratch"
- Applying "remember who you are" and helping kids make decisions in advance
- Using pre-emptive strikes to put the gospel perspective as the foundation
- Creating a book to give your kids on their wedding day (about them)

Solution 2: Remember God's Parenting Patterns

Follow the supreme example of how God parents us.

The best model for parenthood is the one that God Himself has set. He taught us all He could in our premortal home and then gave us our agency. Following God's parenting pattern comes into play as we help our kids learn to work, set goals, be responsible, handle money, make good choices, achieve personal repentance, be motivated and disciplined, and more. Ideas from this chapter include the following:

- Learning and teaching unconditional love
- Applying "hold them close and let them go"
- Understanding agency, choices, and family laws
- Trusting your kids and being trustworthy
- Giving stewardship for clothes, toys, goals, grades, conflicts, choices, values
- Enjoying each other and living for "moments"
- Teaching values
- Appreciating the importance of rituals and traditions
- Identifying angels in your lives and finding joy
- Creating a plan of happiness for your children

Solution 3: Remember Your Direct Channel to Father

Understand that we are mere mortal babysitters who can appeal directly to the real Parent.

What prayer could be more appropriate and more effective than the one that essentially says, "Please help me to understand and raise these, *your* children." There are many opportunities and applications for this special prayer connection regarding rebellion, values, inactivity or apathy, individual discipline, personal prayer, testimony, and more. Ideas from this chapter include the following:

- Applying a powerful and unique kind of stewardship prayer
- Listening and taking notes during prayer
- Praying with your family
- Praying as a couple
- Fearing God and not your kids
- Praying with small children
- Fasting (rejoicing) and prayer
- Improving the atmosphere of your home
- Holding monthly family testimony meetings
- Teaching works and grace

Solution 4: Remember the Church's "Scaffolding"

Take full advantage of all the help, support, and guidance the Church and its programs offer.

Church programs, teachers, advisors, and "the ward family" are there for us, just as we are there for others. They can love and serve our kids, and back up every value and principle we teach. And the prophets sound a sure voice in an uncertain world. This back-up and support from others can be applied to challenges of selfishness and sensitivity, growing up too fast, resolving past mistakes, finding good friends, learning the joy of service, and more. Ideas from this chapter include the following:

- Using the 'general contractor' approach
- Utilizing resources, from teachers to programs
- Helping children memorize and internalize
- Seeing problems with a family-oriented perspective
- Debriefing children after lessons, outings, camps, etc.
- Teaching at dinnertime
- Upgrading family home evenings and scripture study
- Maximizing the Sabbath Day
- Implementing the age of accountability
- Enhancing the teachings from seminary, institute, missions, and the temple

Solution 5: Remember the Savior's Power

Use His Spirit to guide, His Atonement to save, and His priesthood to bless our children.

The Holy Ghost can help us see what our eyes can't, Christ's example and Atonement can guide our every move, and using the priesthood to bless our children and magnify our families brings the actual and literal power of God into our very households and into our children's lives. These advantages can be applied to the challenges of decisions and choices, values, insecurities and depression, ADHD, pornography and sexual experimentation, and more. Ideas from this chapter include the following:

- Understanding priesthood blessings
- Seeking and following promptings
- Creating a spiritual atmosphere in your home
- Using scripture and testimonies as gauges and measures
- Applying the motivating power of the Atonement
- Keeping the Savior foremost, using Christ as a model
- Acknowledging rejoicing and appreciating moments

- Remembering Christ through the sacrament
- Learning from other Christians

AUTHOR'S CLOSING NOTE TO READER

We love you.

We as writers and parents love you as readers and parents.

That may seem a strange way to end this book, especially if you are complete strangers to us.

But it also may be the most direct way to make a point: Being parents is such a huge factor in who you are and who we are, in what we each feel, in what we learn, and in how we think, that it gives us more in common and makes us more similar to each other than any difference that could separate us.

So when we say we love you, we mean that we feel empathy and commonality and concern because we share so much with you by virtue of the fact that we are parents as you are a parent.

And perhaps part of what we all mean when we say we love God is that we understand and appreciate Him more because, for the first time in eternity, we, like Him, are parents.

And if you and we are also members of Christ's restored Church, we share another enormous realm of unity and love.

It is within that sameness and love that we have written this book.

EPILOGUE
For Grandparents and Empty Nest Parents

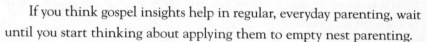

If you think gospel insights help in regular, everyday parenting, wait until you start thinking about applying them to empty nest parenting.

The extended family, the three- or four- or five-generation family, offers endless opportunities to teach and apply the spiritual solutions that can fortify each individual nuclear family and bond and seal them together—like envelopes within envelopes—so that they resemble more and more the family of God.

The stewardship we have of adult children is no less demanding than that of growing children.

The happiest empty nesters and grandparents that we know are the ones who continue to take an active role with their children and grandchildren and who orient themselves more and more to the spiritual side of things.

One of the luxuries of being a grandparent is that the daily duties and hassles of parenting and active, kid-filled households fade away, and we are left with more opportunity to pick and choose what we will teach and what we will concentrate on.

You can begin, as a grandparent and/or an empty nester, to think of yourself more and more as a spiritual advisor. You have earned the right to be that. And it is probably one of the most valuable and important roles you can play with your growing extended family.

You can be the catalyst that brings siblings and aunts and uncles and cousins and all the parts of your family together. You can do it at reunions or you can do it in chat rooms and blogs and other online methods.

It has never been easier to stay in touch with people than it is today. Get on Facebook or send tweets on Twitter like your grandkids do. Meet them in their electronic world just as you invite them to meet you for outings and meetings and reunions in the physical world.

If you want some specific ideas and examples on more active and involved empty nest parenting, go to www.emptynestparenting.com and then adapt any appealing ideas you find there to your personality, your needs, and your family.

ACKNOWLEDGMENTS

We express sincere thanks to Jana Erickson at Deseret Book for her wise suggestions and constant support. Also to Sheri Dew who has encouraged and endorsed this book from the beginning.

To our brilliant friends Stephen and Sandra Covey who have been inspiring mentors for over forty years, we express deep gratitude and enduring admiration.

And to our brave children who have served as guinea pigs most of their lives for our writing, we offer love that feels to us like the closest we have ever come to the pure love of Christ! Particularly we thank our three married daughters—Saren Eyre Loosli, Shawni Eyre Pothier, and Saydi Eyre Shumway—who are astonishing moms (of fourteen glorious grandchildren) and writers in their own right and who each somehow found the time to read and edit this entire manuscript.

NOTES

PERSPECTIVES: *Worldly Challenges, Spiritual Solutions*

1. Harold B. Lee, Conference Report, October 1967, 107.

2. "On the Right Course," from *Cruising Helmsman*, October 1987; found on http://www.netfunny.com/rhf/jokes/87/14917.15.html. Accessed November 18, 2010.

SOLUTION 1: *Remember Your Children's True Identity*

1. Nancy Hanks Baird, "Quench Not the Spirit," BYU Women's Conference, April 30, 2010.

INTERMISSION: *Why It's Worth All the Effort*

1. Harold B. Lee, Conference Report, October 1967, 107.

SOLUTION 3: *Remember Your Direct Channel to the Father*

1. Alfred, Lord Tennyson, "Morte d'Arthur." http://www.online-literature .com/tennyson/723/. Accessed November 18, 2010.

2. This quote has been attributed to St. Augustine, http://thinkexist.com/ quotation/pray_as_though_everything_depended_on_god-work_as/149654. html. Accessed November 17, 2010.

3. Winston Churchill, http://thinkexist.com/quotes/winston_churchill/4.html. Accessed November 19, 2010.

4. Abraham Lincoln, http://www.quoteworld.org/quotes/10275. Accessed November 19, 2010.

Solution 4: *Remember the Church's "Scaffolding"*

1. http:en.wikipedia.org/wiki/It_Takes_A_Village. Accessed November 19, 2010.

2. Gordon B. Hinckley, "First Presidency Message: Taking the Gospel to Britain—A Declaration of Vision, Faith, Courage, and Truth," *Ensign*, July 1987, 7.

3. Words and music by Newel Kay Brown, "I Hope They Call Me on a Mission," *Children's Songbook* (Salt Lake City: The Church of Jesus Christ of Latter-day Saints, 2000), 169. ©1969 IRI.

Solution 5: *Remember the Savior's Power*

1. C. S. Lewis, *The Screwtape Letters* (Philadelphia: Fortress Press, 1980).

2. Parley P. Pratt, *Key to the Science of Theology* (Salt Lake City: Deseret Book, 1978), 61.

3. David A. Bednar, "Watching with All Perseverance," *Ensign*, May 2010, 40–43.

4. C. S. Lewis, *The Lion, The Witch, and the Wardrobe* (Great Britain: HarperCollins, 1950). This was the first book written in the series.

5. Victor Hugo, *Les Misérables* (New York: Washington Square Press, 1964).

INDEX

171